I Am Not the Father

*Narratives of Men Falsely
Accused of Paternity*

M. L. Matthews

TRAFFORD PUBLISHING
BLOOMINGTON, INDIANA

Order this book online at www.trafford.com
or email orders@trafford.com

Most Trafford titles are also available at major online book retailers.

Printed in the United States of America.

ISBN: 978-1-4269-3703-3 (sc)
ISBN: 978-1-4269-3704-0 (e)

*Our mission is to efficiently provide the world's finest, most comprehensive book publishing
service, enabling every author to experience success. To find out how to publish your book,
your way, and have it available worldwide, visit us online at www.trafford.com*

Trafford rev. 7/23/2010

 www.trafford.com

North America & international
toll-free: 1 888 232 4444 (USA & Canada)
phone: 250 383 6864 ♦ fax: 812 355 4082

Table of Contents

Introduction

The narratives in this book are true. Names have been changed to protect the privacy of any innocent parties involved, specifically the children.

I generalized my own personal narrative to protect the feelings and privacy of a family who deals with the aftermath of a severe tragedy every day. I was involved in a paternity case some time ago, and the mother of the child in question died after taking a paternity test, but before the test revealed I was not the father of the child she said I conceived.

I consider that situation tragic on many levels. First, the child in question was never able to develop a relationship with her biological mother. Secondly, that entire family lost a smart, beautiful, loving person. Thirdly, I wonder if the child ever found out who her biological father really is. It is a tragedy if she does not know.

The stories in this narrative need to be told. I've heard it said that there are three sides to every story: His side, her side and the truth. I also realize that an untold story can't be heard. The individual narratives in this project are not attempts to identify good guys and bad guys. The narratives serve as a well-intentioned attempt to understand the experiences of men who were falsely credited with paternity of a child.

The narratives collected for this book are designed to help people understand the experiences of men who were falsely credited with paternity. There are several other conversations that will arise from the collection as well. I suggest that the conversations stemming from the narratives are positive and used to build up and educate rather than being negative and used to break down and berate.

Being falsely accused with paternity has had a tremendous impact on my life. What people see on television or hear on radio talk shows might provide entertaining sound bites, but there is a large degree of context and depth that should be added to the picture. This book provides depth and context.

The narratives are not fictional stories; they are true stories. They are not to be viewed as jokes or pokes at women. They are to be viewed as what they are: narratives of men who were falsely credited with paternity.

I begin the book by responding to the questions I asked the four interview participants and then I narrate my own paternity story. From there, I share narratives from four men I have known personally for up to 26 years.

The four narratives include briefings that talk about how I know the subjects and my expectations for the interview. Each narrative also includes an edited transcript of an audio-recorded interview. The recordings were transcribed verbatim and edited for clarity. The interviews contain adult language that some people might find offensive. I apologize if I offend a reader, but I did not want the interviews edited to the point where they lost their candid quality and authenticity.

The narratives also include reflections. I reflected on each interview during the day or days following the interview to provide an overview of what happened through my lens as the narrator. The reflections also discuss feelings and thoughts from personal experiences that were brought as a result of the interview.

The chapter entitled Conclusions (6) highlights commonalities in the cases and fold in how I identify with the interviewees. It also deals with the impact these cases had on the alleged fathers, my analysis of the interview responses and ways to avoid similar situations in the future.

Chapter 1
My Story

Over-arching question: What are the experiences of men who were falsely credited with paternity?

Talk about the relationship with the person who falsely said I was her child's father...

Question: How did we meet?

My response: I met her walking in the mall.

Question: What was the nature of our relationship? (Committed, casual dating, purely sexual, otherwise)

My response: My relationship with the girl who falsely accused me of paternity started as a typical teenage relationship. We talked on the phone and got to know each other that way.

Question: What were my expectations for the relationship?

My response: I don't know what I expected. In my mind, I met a pretty girl and I wanted to get to know her better. I can't say I had any expectations past that.

Talk about how we spent time together...

Question: What kinds of things did we do?

My response: We talked on the phone.

Question: What kind of atmosphere did the relationship provide me?

My response: The atmosphere was fresh and new. I liked that I had met a girl who didn't go to my high school. She had the sweetest phone voice and we had great conversations. The more we talked, the more we wanted to see one another. The excitement we both shared leading up to our being able to see one another face to face might have contributed to our decision to have sex when we did.

My mom use to caution me about phone dating when I was younger. She didn't want me on the phone for extended periods of time or late at night because she said it would lead to something. I argued that I couldn't do anything wrong through the phone and she argued that I was building desires. She was right. That girl and I were comfortable enough with each other to have sex after talking on the phone for a few weeks. I guess it's not unthinkable. Social websites and date lines have been connecting people who pursue relationships for years.

I went as far as to pay for my own phone line back when I was home with my parents. My mom use to pick up phones throughout the house and listen in on my conversations when I spoke on the house phone. Sometimes she would just listen and at other times she would break into the conversation. That was embarrassing. She told me if I wanted privacy I should purchase my own phone, so I did. Once I got my first job at Fred's Dollar Store in Frayser back in 1996 I would sit in my bedroom and talk on my phone until the early a.m. hours.

Question: What kind of atmosphere do I think the relationship provided her?

My response: I think the relationship provided her with newness and freshness as well. High school students traditionally date students at their high school because school is where they meet people their age. People, whether young or old, get tired of looking at the same faces and talking about the same things. Meeting someone with a fresh face and different conversation adds spice and possibilities.

Over-arching Question: What are the relationships between trust and sexual interactions?

Talk about how much I trusted her....

Question: How honest were you with her?

My response: I was totally honest. I didn't make any promises or commitments to her. Our conversations were about our plans for the future and likes and dislikes. People often lie in relationships when they think telling the truth will bring about negative reactions or consequences. We were just getting to know each other and neither of us had a reason to lie about anything, if there is ever a good reason to lie in the first place.

Question: Aside from lying about the paternity of her child, how honest do you think she was with you?

My response: The relationship was so fresh that she didn't really have any reasons to lie. I can't think of an instance where I felt like she might be lying to me aside from saying I got her pregnant.

Question: How often did you two have unprotected sex with each other?

My response: We used a condom the one time we had sex before she told me she was pregnant.

Question: How did you all decide to have unprotected sex?

N/A

Question: What made you comfortable enough with her to have unprotected sex?

N/A

Question: How did her use of birth control or not factor into your choice to have unprotected sex with her?

N/A

Question: Why did you believe you were the father of her child?

My response: I doubted the child's paternity from the beginning. I thought it was unbelievable that I could get her pregnant from one instance where a condom was properly used. I knew there was a possibility, but I knew it was a slim one.

Question: What did you learn about yourself since you found out you were not the father of her child?

My response: I learned that life can change in an instant. Although I figured I wasn't the child's father, I knew that my priorities would have to change immediately and dramatically if I was proved to be the father.

Question: How did I find out I was not the child's father?

My response: I applied for a paternity test.

Question: What was my reaction to finding out I was not her child's father?

My response: I was stunned. I didn't know what to say or do. I couldn't respond directly to the child's mother because she was dead. I felt confused, angry and free. I knew the child's mother would have a lot of explaining to do for lying if the test showed I was not the father. I never considered the possibility of her dying before everyone knew the truth. I was saddened to know that she wouldn't be around to explain the situation to her daughter. My heart went out to her family as well. They were good people. Although we met on undesirable terms, they welcomed me as part of their family and it seemed, at times, that we all got along. They were probably more hurt than I was, plus I knew they would want answers about the child's paternity that might be hard to find. I was just a teenager trying to understand everything I was going through at the time and not lose focus with school.

Question: How did finding out I was not the father of her child impact my sense of self?

My response: I had to start looking at myself more seriously and through the eyes of the people around me. I reasoned with myself that she said the child was mine because I was the best candidate for fatherhood. I was a nice person who treated her well and I had a bright future ahead of me. I don't know what the other guys in her life had planned for their futures, but I was college-bound and ambitious.

My sense of self had to become sharper. I began to realize that some people would see me as a potential boyfriend or mate and not as a person. I still think the same way now. People react certain ways when they hear my credentials. I've noticed women sizing me up as I talk. I might have seemed like the average guy on first look and maybe they paid me no mind. I could almost hear cranks turning in some women's heads when they hear I'm a single Black man without children or that I have a graduate degree and my own home at the age of 30. To a degree, I have become watchful because I know a woman I might simply want to get to know better might have already determined that I would make a good husband and provider. It's flattering yet scary at the same time.

Question: How did my experience affect your view of women, dating and sex?

My response: My view of women was damaged. I became distrustful and pessimistic. I grew up with only positive views of women because of my relationship with my mother. She was honest, thoughtful, kind and trustworthy. I would have never thought women lie as much as some of them do before my experience. I knew that men were often dishonest in relationships and playing the field was considered cool for men. I never considered the fact that women played the field too, and often times better than men because they had a reputation at stake if they got caught.

I had a bitter taste in my mouth in regards to dating for a while. I was unfaithful and lied consistently in my next few relationships and didn't think it was too bad because I figured that my partner was probably lying to me as well. I was afraid to be open and honest because I didn't want to look like an easy target to believe a lie.

My view of sex didn't change too much. My mother raised me to view sex as an intimate bond shared by married people, but I didn't act according to that knowledge. I had a girlfriend when I was 14 or so and we were both virgins. We attended different schools and talked on the phone almost every day. We had secretly agreed to be each others' first sex partners, but she admitted to losing her virginity to a guy at her high school in their auditorium when I was in the 10th grade. I was devastated and responded by giving up my virginity to one of my schoolmates that same year, 1995. Sex became recreation after that until I was falsely accused of paternity. It would be years before I viewed sex as an intimate special bond again.

Question: What experiences, from then until now, stand out as being the most valuable?

My response: The experience of enduring the constant guilt trips was tremendous. If I had given in and not tested the child's paternity, the child would have never known that I am not her biological father. Children have the right to know their parents, whether the parent is fit and responsible or not. I stuck to my convictions although I was put to the test by the child's mother and her family. I was stronger when it was all over.

Question: What can men and women do to prevent situations like what I experienced?

My response: Honesty is simple in theory, but more difficult in practice. She could have told me there was a possibility I was not the father, but she didn't. On my end, I could have waited until I knew her better before we had sex.

NQ3: How does my experience back then transfer into my everyday experiences now?

Talk about what I will take with me from my experience...

Question: How will I use what I learned from that relationship in my life?

My response: I have to be more careful. Although it might not have been her initial motive to credit me with the paternity of a child whom I did not father, it happened. I know that what happened with us happens a lot, and I don't want to go through that again.

Question: What are the most valuable lessons I will take from my experience?

My response: The most valuable lessons were learning to be more patient and sticking to my convictions when under duress.

Unexpected outcomes:

Talk about changes I made in my personal life, mind-frame and behavior when I thought I was about to be a father...

Question: Why did I make the changes in my life?

My response: The most significant change was my decision not to visit The University of Tennessee at Martin. My father wanted me to attend the University of Memphis instead of Martin anyway, but the thought of having a child at home definitely weighed into my decision.

Question: How did the idea of being a father impact my everyday activities?

My response: I spent more time with the child's mother. We went on dates and shopping for the child together. I got to know her much better after she was pregnant than I had known her before we were intimate.

Question: What is the impact of the changes I made when I thought I was going to be a father, now that I know I am not the father of that child?

My response: The changes I made dealt mainly with the girl who was pregnant at the time. She is no longer with us. Still, I try to keep in mind the importance of getting to know a person before being intimate with them.

I met Kesha when I was a teenager.

I stopped the fair-skinned Coke bottled-shaped young lady as she and a girlfriend walked through the mall. After a brief conversation she gave me her phone number and I called her. We talked on the phone a lot and got to like one another over the next few days. Eventually, we made plans for me to visit her house after school, before her parents got home from work. I went over there and we had sex. I wore a condom that did not bust or slip off.

We talked on the phone a few more times following our sexual episode, but it would be months before we saw each other again.

I randomly called her one day just to see how she had been doing. She seemed happy to hear from me when I called and I was happy to talk to her. She asked a question, though, that changed my entire life the moment she asked it.

I remember it exactly, "What would you say if I told you in six months you would be a daddy?"

I froze. The question left me in shock after not having talked to her for a couple months. I asked her if she was pregnant and she said she thought she might be. She said she hadn't had sex with anyone since me so if she was pregnant I would be the father.

The next day I picked her up from her school and took her to a clinic for a paternity test.

Kesha and a friend of hers got in my car and we were on our way. I sat in the waiting room while she was examined.

My mind was scattered. There were so many thoughts running through my head: "How could she be pregnant? What am I supposed to do now?"

An interesting thing happened in the waiting room, though. Her friend asked me what my problem was, and said I was wrong for having sex with her friend without wearing a condom.

She told me the girl I had slept with asked her if something could "come out" of a penis if it was not "all the way up (erect)."

Kesha's friend's question gave me the impression Kesha had at least attempted sex with another person, but the effort might have been thwarted by the inability to attain a lasting erection. I knew that a pre-ejaculation could have seeped out the guy's penis and into her vagina if there was no condom involved. If that had happened, it would explain why Kesha might have felt she was being truthful when she said she had not had sex with anyone since me. At any rate, I was going to have to know the child was mine before I claimed it, regardless of what might have happened.

I planned to ask about the situation after the pregnancy test, but things started happening at warp speed. Kesha stormed out of the clinic in tears and her friend immediately embraced her. She told me she was indeed pregnant once she calmed down.

I wanted to talk to her, but she fell hysterically into her girlfriend's arms. We got back into my car and she asked me to take her back to school. I wanted to talk to her and asked if I could take her home when we pulled up to her school, but she said she wanted to go back to class. She told me her mother wanted to meet me when I called her later that day.

She said her mom asked her if she was pregnant that day when she got home. I would have to guess Kesha was acting strangely, possibly crying and carrying on at home and her mom knew something was the matter.

I asked her over and over if she had been with another guy and she swore she had not. I even went as far as to create possible scenarios. I remember asking her things like, "Has your vagina been in any contact with a penis since we had sex?" She always said no.

I could do nothing, but wonder if my sperm was the .01 percent that would break through the 99.99 percent protection of a properly worn condom.

A cousin volunteered to go with me to meet her parents. He offered his pistol in case things got out of hand when I told him I didn't need an escort. I told him I didn't want to take his gun either.

I didn't think it would be a violent meeting or that I would need protection. My young mind thought it would be a simple meet and greet.

I remember walking up Kesha's parents' driveway. I wasn't nervous at all. Her step-father was out front working on a car or something. I spoke to him and approached the door afterward. Her mother was cordial. She greeted me with a smile and invited me inside the house. Her stocky older brother stared me down when I walked through the door.

Her step-father came in from outside, sat down in the kitchen and cut right to the chase.

"Now that you've got my daughter pregnant," he bellowed. "What are you gonna do about it?" Without hesitation I replied, "If it's mine, I'm gonna take care of it."

Kesha's brother jumped up and roared out that his sister was not a ho. He was frantic and upset to the point that I wondered if I should have taken my cousin's pistol after all. Kesha's parents thankfully quieted their son and had him leave the room before asking why I offered the answer I did. I explained that we only had one sexual encounter and that I wore a condom that did not bust or come off. On top of that, I mentioned the conversation I held with Kesha's friend in the clinic lobby.

Kesha's mom dismissed her daughter's friend saying something to the degree that she was bad news, didn't know what she was talking about and needed to mind her own business. Kesha's mom also reminded me that condoms are not 100% effective and that females can get pregnant even if her partner wears a condom.

I was confused. I didn't know how to respond aside from insisting on a paternity test. During the course of the conversation, though, I caught Kesha lying to her parents. She told them that we had sex in my house, which was not true. My mother was a housewife and home nearly all the time. Although I would sneak girls into my parents' house back in those days, I only had one chance to do so: on Thursday nights when my mom was at Bible study.

She also told them I took her virginity, but she had told me I was her third sex partner. Hearing her lie to her parents let me know that I couldn't fully trust the things she would say to me.

She insisted I was her child's father that day and for the upcoming weeks and months. What could I do, though? What could I say?

I felt the best thing to do was to give her the benefit of the doubt, wait until the baby was born and have a paternity test.

I was tortured in the meantime. She would call me in the early morning hours and say things like, "The baby just kicked and woke me up so I thought I would call and wake you up."

She would cry about the fact that I didn't trust her enough to call off the paternity test.

Her mother would call me at all hours of the night, too. She would tell me I was wrong for taking her baby's virginity and tossing her to the side.

The guilt trip worked to some degree. I started taking Kesha out on dates, although we never dated before she was pregnant.

My high school basketball coach said he had arranged a workout and visit with the University of Tennessee at Martin's basketball team if I wanted to go. This was an offer I was seriously considering even though I didn't play much of my senior season.

Kesha's family said they wanted her to finish high school while living with me in Martin if I decide to attend college there. I felt like walls were closing in on me. I couldn't believe what was happening to me. I went from a carefree high school student with the whole world ahead of me to a baby daddy with meddling in-laws-to-be.

I decided to attend The University of Memphis on a journalism scholarship. I never even visited UT Martin.

My car transmission gave out just as my freshman year in college had begun. I had to wake up at 5 a.m. to catch a 5:30 bus from my home in Frayser to the downtown bus terminal. From downtown I would transfer to another bus that dropped me at The University of Memphis. Kesha or her mom might call me on any given night crying, ranting or raving at 2 or 3 a.m. during that time.

I never snapped, though. I never told Kesha's mom that her daughter told me she wasn't a virgin or that I had sex in her house. I remember thinking to myself that the air would be clear once we took the test.

I still remember the day the child was born. I had another car by this time. I called Kesha's house to check on her and her sister-in-law told me Kesha had gone into labor earlier that morning. I spoke to my professor Dr. Hopson, who gave me permission to be absent from class and I rushed to the hospital. A beautiful baby girl had been born by the time I got there.

I held her and smiled, but I didn't sign the birth certificate. Her parents were outwardly bothered by the fact I didn't sign, but I didn't let it intimidate me. Actually, I asked for a paternity test then and there, but was told by the nurse that I would have to go through a private doctor or the courts.

Kesha and the baby were released from the hospital soon thereafter. I stopped by her parents' house and picked the baby up. I took her to my parents' house to show my family. My mom and younger brother were there. My older brother and Pop came to the house once I called them.

Everyone held her. She was a pretty red baby with curly hair and dimples. I fell for her, too. My daddy held her briefly and said he didn't want to see her again until he saw the paternity test results. He also cautioned me not to get attached to the child too soon.

Kesha's parents said they were going to arrange the test, but had not done so in months so I went downtown and applied for a paternity test myself.

Kesha and I were summoned to court. When we got there, the child, her mother and I were orally swabbed and photographed. The test results would be revealed two months later in court. I focused on school in the meantime.

Out of nowhere tragedy struck. I found out Kesha had been killed in a random accident before we got the paternity test results. It was about 6 a.m. when her mother woke me up with a phone call to tell me her daughter died that morning.

My heart stopped. I couldn't believe it. The pretty little girl I met in the mall, was intimate with, and might be the mother of my child, was dead.

I visited with her family. Some of the family knew about the paternity issue and treated me in an unfriendly manner while others were compassionate. Her mother shared diary entries that talked about my relationship with her. The letters said she didn't understand why I doubted her and that she knew I was the father of her child.

Some of her family seemed to hate me and Kesha resented my asking for a paternity test. My own conscience bothered me too. I wanted to be fair although I knew the likelihood of me being the father was slim. Up until her death, Kesha never stopped trying to convince me the child she carried in her womb and birthed belonged to me. I was also dealing with my father's drug addiction, that he later overcame, and my mother's schizophrenic episodes along with adjusting to college on top of all that. Not to mention, my entire family was recovering from my brother Marland's murder September 14, 1996. It would be a gross understatement to say I was dealing with a lot of stress.

An aunt and uncle accompanied me to the funeral where I was introduced as the child's father. I needed their support because I was being viewed as a real villain and deadbeat dad. I received evil stares from many of the people at the funeral.

Interestingly enough, my aunt was convinced the child was mine when she saw her. The child had a fair complexion, much like mine, and she had dimples as do I. I remember my aunt joking that we were going to keep the baby whether she was mine or not because she was so cute.

The results were ready and we were to return to court a month later.

I remember sitting anxiously in the courtroom that day. Kesha's parents came in their deceased daughter's behalf. Kesha's mom, step-dad, the child and I sat together. My name was called and I was asked to approach the bench.

The judge revealed I was not the child's father and I was free to go. My heart dropped. I didn't know how to feel. Without thinking I looked to the baby and her grandparents. I read the lips of a distressed grandmother as they mouthed the words, "that ain't right. (She) wasn't with nobody else." Her husband dropped his head slightly. He gave me a look that was half hurt from his heart and half apology to me when he looked up. I was hurt and relieved at the same time.

I was told I was always welcome at their home, but it was too uncomfortable for everyone around when I attempted to visit. I went there once or twice before deciding not to complicate things any further. I felt sorry for the child who would grow up having never met her deceased mother. I also wondered how I would explain who I was if I stuck around. I wondered, too, how her family would explain why she didn't have a father around. Sometimes I wonder if I will have to explain to some young girl one day that I am not her father.

Chapter 2
Sax Player

Chip's Briefing

My home (Memphis)

May 18, 2010. Noon.

Chip is on the way to my place for the first interview in the narrative. I feel like I'm going on a job interview or like it's almost tip-off time for a high school basketball game. I'm not nervous; I'm excited.

This project means a lot to me on several levels, and I want to do this right. I've been writing since second grade and I still love it. I've always enjoyed telling stories. I remember when my dad took me to see the Teenage Mutant Ninja Turtles movie back in the '90s. I got home and recounted the entire movie from beginning to end to my friend Renauldo, who lived across the street.

Chip volunteered for involvement in this project. I didn't even know he had gone through his experience before I decided to write this book. I randomly texted him to ask what he thought about the idea of me narrating the plights of three guys I grew up with who were falsely credited with paternity in the past. His response to my text was that I should interview him too.

I immediately called him to get details. He told me that the child he had introduced to me as his son months earlier was not his son after all. I was taken by surprise and could only laugh. I congratulated him on his newfound freedom and explained the purpose of the "I Am Not the Father" project. Approximately one to two months later, May 18, 2010, here we are.

Chip's Interview

Tell me about your relationship with the person who falsely said you were her child's father...

Chip: "Umm, (clears throat) well. What do you really want to know about the relationship?"

Me: How did you two meet?

Chip: "Work. We used to work at Fed Ex together, man, out there in the hub. And she was just, she was cool people. We were on a team together, worked a couple of times together or whatever and ya know, we just started kickin' it after work."

Me: When was that?

Chip: "This was like... I wanna say... I probably met her around about February or March of '07."

Me: What was the nature of your relationship with her?

Chip: "We were just cool. You know somebody you work with. You know me. I'm a flirtatious kinda guy. Ya know so I probably kinda flirted with her a little bit. And we just took it a little step further ya know. It wasn't nothing just serious. We went out a couple of times and one thing led to another, and we just started kickin' it."

Me: So what were your expectations when y'all started kickin' it?

Chip: "I wasn't trying to get in nothing serious. If it was to happen it was just gonna happen. That wasn't nothing I was searching for at the time. I'm an in-the-flow kinda of guy. If it happens, it happens. If it don't, it don't."

Me: What kind of things did y'all do?

Chip: "I mean, ya know, we went out, went to the movies, went out to eat. Just normal stuff, kickin' it. It wasn't like, umm... I wouldn't bring her around friends. It was basically just me and her just kickin' it, goin' out, just getting to know each other."

Me: Tell me about any date, just a specific date.

Chip: "Umm… (long pause) I can say… (another pause). We went to the movies, went and chilled, watched a movie. Then later probably go back to the crib or something. Ya know, chill, talk and you know how that goes. Ya know what I'm sayin?' At the end of the night it's just something that happened."

Me: Ok. What kind of atmosphere did the relationship provide for you?

Chip: "Initially… it was carefree. It was just something for me to do. And then you know with anything, as you put time in you catch emotions or at least care about it. And then it became a little more fun cuz this is a person I know lil bit better and I feel like I can chill with. And then ya know… later on down the line stuff started.

"As you really get to know a person… If you take the time to really pay attention to little small details and analyzing situations, you start to see things you don't like that maybe would frustrate you down the line that you use to laugh at. You're like, 'I really don't like that, but I really don't wanna try to change that because that's you.' And then you see yourself not being able to adjust to the situation as comfortably as you would like to. So then it becomes stressful."

Me: Tell me a story about a time when something you might have laughed at, it wasn't funny no mo.

Chip: "Like umm … We gonna go to the point when we found out she was pregnant. We can go down that line.

"We would go kick it at my mom's house and a lotta people would be there. At this point when I found out she was pregnant. I took the initiative to be like, 'We need to make this work because it's a baby involved now.'

"So we would go kick it at my mom's house and she would go off to the back. Or just hang out and not be around nobody. And at first it was like, 'okay, maybe she don't wanna interact or whatever.' Then it got to the point, I was like, 'you know that is becoming a problem because you excluding yourself from everything that's goin' on. And you talking about people don't want to talk to you, but you not in there where they can talk to you.'"

Me: Ok. What kind of atmosphere do you think the relationship made for her?

Chip: "(Pauses….takes a deep breath) hmmm… I say secure."

Me: Why would you say that?

Chip: "Because anybody knows me knows that I'm passionate. I care. If I'm gonna give something, I'm gonna give it my all and I'm gonna be real passionate about it. And I'ma care for it. I'ma make sure it's taken care of in the right order. Like, I'ma guard it, like basically with my life to make sure it stays intact. So, I guess she saw that and was like, 'well, he's a good guy; maybe now it could be like… he may not do me like other guys have done me.' So maybe in her eyes she said I can be secure with him. He will make sure that everything is good on his end and if it's good on his end it will be good on my end."

Me: What did she do to give you that impression? What makes you think she felt like that?

Chip: "Looking back, seeing everything that happened… I may have not been analyzing it at the time it was going on, but now looking back and seeing things that happened with us … a couple of months ago and a year ago, up until when we broke up. From then until now, I'm seeing things and noticing little things I had picked up on earlier were still things later that I could sense."

Me: Tell me about it…

Chip: "I'm actually cool with a guy she used to talk to, and we are in so many ways similar. He was saying stuff and I was like, 'Dang, dawg. I'm the same way.' I was like, 'That's probably why she couldn't fool with us, because we were too…'

"Maybe she wasn't used to having a guy that's really caring and acts like he wants to be there for her or whatever. She basically brushed him off the same way she did me.

"She started being insecure … because she thought I was too good to come by, if it makes sense. So it's like she misses out on things because she tries to… (Pause) find the negative in it. She's like, when anything is going to good, it's got to be something bad. So (she) gonna push it out to see what it is. Then when it don't get there she wasted her time. At that point, the guy is frustrated and he doesn't wanna be there. So, it's like, when she has security, she knows she's good, she thinks it can't last too long. And she tries force the negativity on the situation to try to make it… to see if it's false or if it's what she thought it was going to be."

Me: How did she force the negativity?

Chip: "Out the blue. You know if you go digging for something hard enough you will find something. So it's like little, little stuff. Ya know I'ma saxophone player, and I got gigs. So being that the sax is a sexy instrument, ya know you gotta have feelings and emotions behind it. So you got a female looking at you in the crowd, you just can't be all stuck up while you're playing and not look at her and not smile at her. And my ex-girlfriend would see that and take it as, 'you're trying to get with her, you're trying to flirt with her, you're trying to take her home.'

"No. I was being a good musician. I was being an entertainer. I was trying to make sure she enjoyed herself so when I have another show she can come back. But we used to have arguments about what I did. That's what I do, playing the saxophone. I'm not gonna stop. So, you got a have a problem with what I do and how I do it, you got a problem with me. And as much as I tried to stay calm about it and talk to her about it she never wanted to see it. She never wanted to believe that's what was actually going on."

Me: Let's talk a little bit about trust and how it relates to sexual interaction. How honest were you with her?

Chip: (Pause) I was totally honest.

Me: Ok. Give me an example of you being totally honest with her.

Chip: "When we started talking we were like... (Starts new sentence) You know how everybody gotta get that, that... (Starts again) I'm a guy for understanding. If we got an understanding up front, I feel like that's the foundation for the rest of the relationship. So when we started talking she had just gotten out of a bad relationship and I wasn't looking for no relationship. I was like, "I just wanna kick it." And I meant that when I said it. I just wanted to kick it and have fun, ya know what I'm sayin? You can't be out here alone and not enjoying life. I said, 'Cause yesterday has already happened. It's what you are going to do about tomorrow. You can't sit there and be mad about yesterday because what happened yesterday made you mad. What you gonna do about today?'

"So I'm the type of guy that's progressive and trying to move past whatever happened that hurt me in the first place. I tried to let her know that's how I was. I told her, and I presented it like that. That's when she opened up and said we can go kick it and we can go do this, have fun and not think about other stuff. It wasn't that I was trying to get with (her) or be with (her). I just wanted to go kick it. The first couple times we kicked it, that's all we did was kick it. And I guess it got to a point where, ya know, sexual feelings got involved in it. That's when it happened."

Me: Aside from her lying about the paternity of the child, how honest do you think she was with you?

Chip: "Ok. See now... now, I can say that she wasn't honest at all. I took the time to analyze the situation and pay attention to everything she said. So like now, I can say she wasn't honest, but initially I saw a little deception, but I don't see much. You can tell when (someone) is lying about some things or lying about a lotta stuff. As far as the baby thing, when she brought it to me I factored in everything that could have happened. And I was like, 'okay this could be.' Like when she gave me the weeks and all. It's a high chance (the baby) could be mine. Ya know what I'm sayin' so, I wasn't the type of person that would say, 'Aw hell naw, that ain't mine.'

"I sat there and said, 'you said you (are how far along)?' And I thought back and I was like okay. Well maybe... Damn, I fucked up. Maybe it is mine and shit like that my bad (Pip apologized for the profanity. It seemed as if he was re-living the moment he found out she was pregnant).

"So, when she told me, I was like damn, it's mine. And how she told me, ya know what I'm saying, because at this point we were kickin' it tough. We weren't together, but I mean, if somebody asked me to go out somewhere that would be the person I would call. But if she said naw, then I might go to another option. It was one of those situations. Now... it's not a given that I was gonna bring her, but that's my first option. At that point that's what it was."

Me: You mentioned at the beginning you noticed a little deception, what was that?

Chip: "Like I said. We were working together and I'm flirtatious. When I first meet her she did have a guy, she had a boyfriend. We didn't ever do nothing, but I mean we on the job and you still flirting with me at the end of the day, ya know what I'm saying? Now, he might not get mad because we have not done anything, it was no touching, no hugging, none of that. But body language speaks in volumes as well, even though you can't hear it, it's something about the way you move and how you give off that vibe to somebody. She wasn't deceiving me because I was nobody. In retrospect she didn't deceive me, but she did have a boyfriend."

Me: Ok, you said later, you could see that she lied a lot, tell me about that.

Chip: Like… (pauses) whatcha mean?

Me: You said that at first there was a little deception and then looking at it… (Chip started to speak)

Chip: "Yeah, looking back…Man, this is crazy… (This seems like it could be the first time Pip thought back to specific instances where he was deceived. His face looked like he was connecting the dots in his brain and all of a sudden he looked as if a light bulb turned on over his head).

"Alright, the child in question turned two recently. Up until a couple months ago this child lived with me because he was my child. But at his first birthday party which was only a year ago… We had the party on that Saturday… But almost a year ago we had a birthday party for him and she left the house and said, 'I'm going to get my cousin.'

"She comes back with two kids and an adult, a male. This guy didn't come into the house at all. He didn't do too much of nothing. And at the time I didn't have the child. It was his birthday party so he was outside playing. And while she was gone I had to be the adult at the party because it's my child's birthday party. We were at her house, by the way, at my child's birthday party, so I had to make sure everything was going smooth. So when she got back I was just chillin', being cordial, talking to the parents, and making sure the kids were having fun. And I saw him. And I spoke. I was like 'whassup?' She was like yeah this is my cousin Pat.

"She didn't tell me about the little kids she brought. I just noticed that they came with them. So I'm like 'aw okay. Whassup bruh?' He said whassup. Now still, I ain't think about it cuz, I mean, me and her not together first of all. She got a boyfriend that I know of, so I felt like she didn't have to lie to me about nothing, ya know what I'm saying?

"I came in, now you didn't have to have the party at your place but you did to make it seem like you was the bigger parent, the better parent. I was (thinking) 'everybody that knows you know that you don't have your child, so I was like I don't really care, I will come.' So I'm thinking she don't gotta lie.

"Now the next month… you know I told you I play the saxophone. I had a lil gig downtown that I had to do a sound check for at like two in the afternoon and I saw her car. And I saw the dude with the dreads that she said was her cousin.

"So I called her and was like 'so where you at?' she said 'I'm at work.' I'm like, 'aw for real?... aw man. I thought I saw your car.'

(Female) 'Naw.'

(Chip) 'Are you sure?'

(Female) 'Where you at?'

(Chip) 'Downtown and I coulda sworn I just saw your car. You the only one that got the (sports car) with the (specific emblem) on the back'... It's so distinctive.

(Female) 'Aw yeah. My friend got my car.'

(Chip) 'Your friend got your car?'

(Female) 'Yeah.'

(Chip) 'Aw for real?... So you must be in his car today?'

(Female) 'Uh... I don't talk to him no mo.'

(Chip) 'Wait a minute. whoa, whoa, whoa, I just saw you two weeks ago and this nigga was at your house, whatcha mean you don't talk to him no mo?'

(Female) 'You know it was some crazy stuff. My little boy made a mistake and called him your name and he got mad talking about we were still fuckin' off so I had to... something, something ("Something, something" represents Pip not remembering the end of her response)...so we just stopped talking.'

(Chip) That was bullshit cuz dude knows me. We done had a conversation with each other so I know that ain't the case. I said, 'aw for real,'

(Female) 'Yeah, but (another) friend is in my car now.'

"I didn't say nothing, I recognized the guy from the party with the dreads that were really distinctive. You can't forget a face like that.

"I said okay and I let it play cool for a long time, about another two months. I had to go by her house and get the baby because she didn't want to bring him or she wanted me to do something, so I waited, she wasn't at home. So they pull up, it's her and him. I'm like, 'aw whassup up?'

"She didn't introduce us. She ain't do nothing, she just kept walking and didn't nobody say nothing.

(Chip) 'Ain't that your cousin?'

(Female) 'Naw.'

(Chip) 'It ain't?'

(Female), 'Naw.'

(Chip) 'His name is Pat, right?'

(Female) 'Yeah.'

(Chip) 'Aw okay.' I said, 'So that's your nigga now?'

(Female) 'why?'

(Chip) 'Cuz at the birthday party that was your cousin.'

She hesitated and looked.

(Female) 'I told you them kids were my cousins.'

(Chip) 'What kids? I didn't even know you brought any kids.'

(Female) 'You didn't see them two little kids that came back when I came back?'

"Now, all of a sudden she remembers the story, ya know what I'm sayin'? She remembered how she introduced me and was like… 'boy whatever. Anyway…you ready?'

"She tried to change the subject real quick. And I noticed how when I confronted her about it her voice elevated… If I were the type of guy to just get real mad and just smack a bitch, I would be wrong. Cuz she just sat there and lied to me, ya know what I'm sayin'?

"After that point then, I started thinking. Why would she lie and tell me that's her cousin? Cuz if you fuckin' off on your nigga, I ain't got nothing to do with that cuz I ain't your nigga.

"I'm just your baby daddy, right?

"This is the other thing that got me. Like I said this was June, so you know Father's Day is in June. And this was only my second Father's Day being celebrated at the time.

"So ya know, I'm like okay, 'so you gonna bring (my son) to church?'

(Female) 'Yeah, I'll bring him…'

"She didn't come to church.

(Chip) 'What happened to you bringing him?'

(Female) 'I overslept.'

"I said whatcha mean you over slept? I coulda came and got him. You didn't call and say nothing. You didn't text me or nothing. Ya know what I'm sayin'?

"I don't know what's going on. I'm worried cuz yall ain't came by. She didn't say nothing. So I had another church to play at that evening. So I was like, 'am I going to get to see him today?'

"She said, 'yeah. I will bring him when you get out of church.'

"I said, 'okay.'

"So I called when I got out of church.

(Chip) 'Where y'all at?'

(Female) 'We at Pat mama house.'

(Chip) 'Y'all at Pat mama house? So what you tryna say? So I can't see my lil boy?'

"Then she got an attitude with me... So I'm like, 'you at Pat mama house on Father's Day, but you had no reason to come by my house on Mother's Day, but you came by...'"

Me: Let me ask you this, Pat, is that the boyfriend she had when you met her at FedEx?

Chip: "No that's a different person, a different guy."

Me: The boyfriend from FedEx, where is he now...at that time, were they still together, do you know?

Chip: "The boy from FedEx...she had another child and that's his father."

Me: Ok...

Chip: "And that's all I can say about that, that's his father. He wasn't around much when I was there taking care of my lil boy and his lil boy at the same time."

Me: How often did y'all have unprotected sex?

Chip: "Well, initially, before she got pregnant, not at all. But the story everybody tells that most folks don't believe is that the condom broke, it did. Not just once, the first time, I stopped and put another one on. But this particular time it broke in the craziest time ever.

"And you know most folks say when you wear a rubber you still pull out? Maannnn... sometimes you just can't. And when it broke, I felt it break, and I also felt me... I was like, 'damn.' But I was like, 'ok maybe we...it might not happen...maybe we safe.'

"And even after that I was using a rubber, ya know what I'm saying? When she told me she was pregnant I was like, 'damn.' I didn't tell her the rubber broke either. So for her to tell me she was pregnant, left me to believe that it could only be mine because, how you end up pregnant if you talkin' bout you ain't fucked wit nobody else and you only fucking me? And I knew the rubber busted."

Me: So, the condom busted at the point of ejaculation?

Chip: "Right."

Me: Okay

Chip: "So once she became pregnant there was no point in wearing a rubber no more, I can't get her pregnant no more... (Chip and I laugh). That's how I looked at it. I mean, just bein' real."

Me: Yeah. So let's fast forward a lil bit. How did you find out that you were not the father of the child?

Chip: "How did I find out for certain or how did I find out? How did I have proof that I wasn't the father or how did I have any idea that I wasn't?"

Me: Either one. Start at either place...

Chip: "Well, I figured the baby wasn't mine, after...maybe toward the end of 09. Just little shit that started happening. We were doing good. Like I said, the baby was living with me, and on the weekends she would have him and it got to the point where she would umm,... she stopped bringing him over herself, she started having Pat bring him to the house cuz she was late for work. Then she was talking about...like now she saying, 'I couldn't call you because I know you would be doing this and you would be doing that.'

"And I said, 'you have never been able to not call me and me not come get him.' So I said 'that stuff you talking is nothing, you can't give me that'... (Pip asked me at this point, 22 minutes into the interview, if he could be himself. Although he had been using profanity from time to time he was being careful to guard his language. I encouraged him to speak as naturally as possible. I knew some of his anger and frustration might show through his language, but I did not want to censor him to the point that he couldn't tell his story comfortably).

"I said, 'cuz that shit you talking ain't nothing so don't even give me that bullshit, acting like I'm not gone be here to take care of my child. Because since (the child's birth) if you ever picked up the phone and called me I was always there for everything. So you can never say that I wouldn't come get him.'

(Female) 'Well you know I just was running late and I was gonna have to wait for you to get there.'

(Chip) 'I don't give a fuck. That's my child and your child. Take the time out. Get up early enough to do what you gotta do. Don't make that no excuse cuz you got another nigga dropping my child off. That's the only time me and you communicate. You don't answer the phone when I call and you don't call me. So, you taking the little time that we got to talk away.'

"She didn't look at it like that. So I didn't even say nothing else. I asked her why you don't call to check on your child, she was like, 'well, cuz I know he in good hands.'

(Chip) 'What the fuck? That's still your child.'

"So it was getting to the point that she couldn't ever look at me eye to eye. Or if we did talk about something we had to argue. So I'm like, 'what's the point, why are we doing this?'

"So I started analyzing shit. Then one time my mama came to me and said this is out the blue now. She said, 'that's who they say the baby's daddy is (referring to Pat).'

"My mama didn't even talk to her folks. My mama didn't even know her folks. Just out the blue my mama said that shit. So... (pause) I ain't gonna say I'm not spiritual because I am. I been going to church my whole life and I know one thing I have always heard.

"'Pray about it, pray about it.' And if you wanna know, ask God about it and He will tell you everything you need to know about it, that's what I know. So, I did. I prayed about it.

"At first, I wasn't saying the right prayer. I was asking to remove the doubt from my heart, to stop that because it was just the devil working on me. That's what I was saying.

"He removed it from my heart but it was still in the world. Ya know everybody was still saying it and I'm like, 'whatever, whatever, whatever.'

"Then I thought, 'I need some revelation on this subject because once I get it, it will be out of the dark.' There's no way for me to not know. I asked Him, and I left it alone.

"All I knew was that he was my child and I was gonna take care of him. But I still saw signs that could turn (the child) away from me. Like he wasn't looking like me as much. But, ya know, he still mines cuz I had been taking care of him for so long. Then umm ... the end of January came.

"She came to pick him up one Friday and the Monday she was supposed to bring him back, she didn't call. She didn't do nothing. It was like 12 o'clock, now I normally get him like 8:30 on Mondays. So I call and she was like, 'well I'ma keep him today.'

"I was like, 'why you didn't tell me?'

"She was like, 'I don't know.'

"Why would she tell me I don't know? Why wouldn't she give me a real reason, except the I don't know shit? That shit used to irk my fuckin' nerves. It's like she use to be trying to get to me, but I never let it get to me.

"I was like, 'aite, whateva.' I said, 'are you bringing him tomorrow?'

(Female) 'I don't know.'

(Chip) 'What? Look, stop playing, what's going on?'

"She didn't say... nothing. But she would call my mama and tell my mama everything I need to know. She would be like, 'yeah I'ma keep him his week. I don't have to work and he ain't feeling good. I'ma take him to the doctor.'

"(Chip with frustration wearing on him as he recalled those conversations) Why you couldn't tell me that when I called you to ask about him? Or when I say something you gotta try to argue with me cuz I'm asking too many questions? Ain't that what a father supposed to do, to be concerned about his child, right?"

Me: So how did you find out technically?

Chip: "After that Monday, I didn't see him for a whole month... And I was like, man I'm getting tired of this shit. Folks were like you need to go down to juvenile court and do this and that. So I went to juvenile court and they told me that it wasn't anything I could really do because she is the mama and even though she was supposed to be paying me child support I didn't really have custody of the child. She just owed me for everything I paid for and the fact that I was still taking care of the child. So, that next week I went to her aunt's house.

"So, umm, I was like, 'man what's going on? Y'all talk to (the child's mother)?' Cuz when they saw me they were (looking at me) like 'why are you here?'

"I was like, 'what's wrong? I ain't talked to (her) and I ain't seen (my son) in a month. She got her number changed and she done moved so I ain't got no way to contact her. When have y'all talked to her?'

"They were like, 'Well, we have talked to her and she came by.'

"They tried to act like they aint have no (telephone) number on her.

"I said, 'where she at?'

"They said they didn't know.

"So, I'm just sittin' there. I ain't no fool. Something was gonna come up. They were gonna get tired of seeing me or something. She was gonna come by, something was gonna happen, I just knew something was gonna happen.

"Her cousin came through the door and he didn't recognize me. He was like, 'mane, who is you?'

"They like, 'that's (the child's) daddy.'

(Cousin), 'Ay bruh what's going on?'

(Chip), 'I ain't seen (my son).'

(Cousin) 'You wanna talk to him bruh?'

(Chip) 'They sound like they aint no number on (his mother).'

(Cousin) 'Bruh! You wanna talk to her?'

Everybody got quiet. They was like, 'oh lord,' shakin' they heads.

(Chip) 'Mane, yeah. Let me talk to her.'

"Cuz, before I went over there, this is what I said to myself. Actually, I told my cousin. We were sittin' there smoking a blunt.

"I was like, 'I don't think that little boy is mine. It's too much going on right now and something is telling me that he aint mine. I don't want a test though. I don't wanna pay for them to tell me he ain't mine cuz I'm gonna snap. If I get a test, she gotta be there while I get the results and I know if they tell me in her face that their 99.9% sure that I'm not the father, I'll just be in jail…that's real shit.'

"So I called her, we argued and we talked.

(Chip) 'So what's going on?'

(Female) 'What's up?'

(Chip) You the one been calling me from a private number talking about you wanna talk, so let's talk.'

"She was fidgety with her words or whatever. So I asked, 'What you trying to say I can't see my son no mo?'

(Female) 'That's on you.'

(Chip)…what?…what kind of shit is that to say to the daddy? "I been taken care of him for two years, how you gonna say that that's on me?

(Female) 'Cuz he ain't yours.'

"That's what she said. That's how she said it."

Me: What did you do from that point?

Chip: "Hung-up the phone. Then I was like, 'you know what?' So I called back. She didn't pick up. So I'm still at her folks' house. I sat there for a minute. I had to take that shit in. I looked at her aunt and said… 'she said he aint mine.'

(Aunt) Aw, Chip. Don't believe that. Don't believe it.'

"I wanted to call her a bitch to her face cuz bitch you done let me sit in your house and you know the business."

Me: So, how did the paternity test come about?

Chip: "So, after I left her aunt's house she called."

(Female) 'You aite?'

(Chip) 'I really ain't got shit to say to you, but are you lying to me? If you not lying, obviously you got proof and if you got some proof, then I want to see it.

(Female) 'Okay.'

(Chip) 'What you doing? You ain't no excuse not to come by my house and bring me the mother fuckin' papers.'

"She didn't come. So I called the next day and said, 'what's up? I want them papers.'

(Female) 'I'm at work.'

(Chip) 'What time you go on break? I'll come get 'em. Tell your nigga to bring em cuz I know he got your car, and I'll meet y'all.'

I went up there and got the papers."

Me: And what did they say?

Chip: "It said in the case of (said child), and all the other shit they say… Patrick M. M. is 99.999% the biological father."

Me: How did you feel?

Chip: "I saw my name and another nigga's name as the father of my name… That ain't no shit a nigga wanna see.

"You know it was like damn. So, I read it right there. We were standing face to face. The only reason I didn't smack her, cuz I was high as hell. I'm not even gonna lie to you… Blunts to the face, I had to…

"Cuz I had been taking care of a child for two years. (There was) nothing really to stop me from killing (her). Not to say that I would have, but you know what I'm saying, most niggas think like that.

"But I had to think about it. I asked for it. I asked for that paper. Not initially from her, but I asked for it. So, He (God) wouldn't have told me if He wasn't prepared for me to be ok with it.

"I mean physically, I was hurt. But spiritually, that's what I wanted.

"It took me about a week and a half to two weeks to understand that I asked for that. I never called her out of her name. I never called her a bitch...when I got the paper I was like, 'so...you've been knowing?

"Cuz the paper said Feb. 5th...Feb. 1st when they got tested which means you knew all of January that you were going to get tested. Because obviously she didn't have any money and you gotta pay money to get this test. Just a couple of weeks ago, you were asking me to buy you some Pampers.

"I get pampers for you for the weekend and you still bring him home without pampers. Obviously, you been knowing, cuz you saved up for this test.

"Why couldn't you come to me like a woman about it? This is the stuff I'm talking about. I asked you from the front, would you would always be 100 with me?

"I knew something might go down. But at the end of the day, all I wanted is for you to talk to me like an adult. I'm not one of these niggas in the streets that's gonna get mad and get real stupid. You be an adult and I will be an adult. If you come to me like an adult I'ma talk to you like an adult.

"I bet you expected everything in me to do something to you, but I ain't got time for that. That ain't gonna change what's on this paper.

"For two whole years you lied to me about my child that you let me take care of and you been with his daddy all the time.'

(Female) 'I didn't know.'

(Chip) 'When did you find out?'

(Female) 'We was talking about it one day...

(Chip) 'Y'all was talking about it one day? Well damn. You couldn't talk about it with me?...so you fucked the nigga while you were fuckin' me and you wasn't 100 from the beginning?'

(Female) 'It wasn't. It wasn't'...

(Chip) 'Man whatever. So you been knowin', basically? This the same nigga from the birthday party.'

"I just broke it down to her to let her know that I know you been lyin' to me. Ain't nothing you can say to get me to believe that you were not lyin' to me from the jump. She just sat there with a little shit face, know what I'm saying?"

Me: So what was your relationship with her after that day?

Chip: "After that, I ain't have shit to say to her. My whole thing was I'ma get my name off that birth certificate, and….I'm through with it."

Me: What about the money you spent?

Chip: "I can't do nothing about that… I mean, in my defense, I was doing what I was supposed to do as a father… See a lot of people might say, 'nigga you stupid. You shoulda got a DNA test in the beginning.'

"Why did your daddy get one with you?

"If your daddy woulda told you he got a DNA test, how would you feel? How would you look at him?

"My daddy wasn't there for me. So, I made a promise to myself at the age of 12 that I would never do a child like that, ever. I'm not going to not be there for my child.

"I'm not gonna have my child waking up asking his mama, 'mama why daddy ain't here? Why he ain't come to play with me? Do he not care? He don't love me?'

"Them questions I asked my mama. I don't want nobody to ask they mama that. Cuz I know how that feels to look into your mama's eyes and for her to just sit there and say, 'baby I don't know. He gone.' … Just being real."

Me: So, what you grew up going thru and what you just went thru the last two years, how has that affected your view of women, dating and sex?

Chip: "I look at it like this man. Everything is learning experience, but like I said I can't sit here and blame the future for the past. I still gotta go day to day…I know what happened and I gotta take my precautions, but I can't fault a girl now that I'm really feeling, that I know I can give my all too because of something you did to me two years ago. I can't really say that every female is scandalous… Everybody ain't the same. Everybody go through things differently and everybody look at things differently. And, I mean, I go back and look at things, we weren't serious, so I wasn't a saint in that situation and what was goin' on."

Me: What experiences stand out to you as the most valuable?

Chip: "I learned a lot about myself. I mean a lot of people come to me saying, 'for a 23yr old, you seem to have your head on right and you know what you wanna do. And by you not having a college degree you seem to really know what you want and how to get it.'

"That just told me that I had no excuse for not being there. I was gonna get up every day and grind hard to make sure he ate, so in that respect I stopped focusing on me and tried to have a better life for him. And if I had to better myself in the process, then that was just what it was gonna take. But he wasn't going to see the struggle. All he would know is that daddy was there taking care of me."

Me: What do you think men and women can do to prevent those types of situations?

Chip: "Shit, be honest. That's the only thing I can say... that's what it buckles down to, being honest and talking and not being in such a rush to have sex, know what I'm sayin'? Get to know a person before to start that situation with them...

"It's cool that she affected me, my life, my situation...but you have a child involved. So not only did you lie to me, you lied to your child... She also affected the life of her child.

"Your child is gonna grow up, and whatchu gonna tell him? 'Mama was a ho. I was fucking with him and him at the same time? I named you him, but shit, this is your daddy?'

"What the hell? So it's like you gotta think about all the variables, it ain't just two people in that equation...it's a whole bunch.

"You fuckin' with a family too, my family thought that this was their child, ya know?...So you done touched a lot of lives. Not to mention the kids that got attached to this child that don't understand the fact that, 'aw he not your son no more, Chip?...how that work?'

"So, the only thing I can say is just be honest and don't sit there and lie to that person cuz you lying to yourself."

Me: How would you use what you learned for the rest of your life?

Chip: "I can't let it change me. Like actually this situation has gotten me... I've been blessed since this situation. It was what I would call... you know everybody goes through their trials and tribulations. That was my trial. He tested me. Obviously I passed. He was ready for me to get out. So all I can do is when I'm faced with another situation is keep my head up, stay afloat, don't let it bring me down and do what I have to do to get through it."

Me: You mentioned earlier that you made some changes in your life, what kinds of changes?

Chip: "Like, I'm an only child so my whole life has been only about me, up until the fact that I was going to be a father, or at least I thought I was going to be a father. And at that point I had to think: 'Okay. It's no longer about me. I gotta do for me, but I gotta do more for him.' And not only that, my thing was, I know children cling to their parents, especially their mothers, so if she was hurting he was hurting so I had to be there to take care of her too. So it's like I just buckled down and realized what was important and it wasn't me, basically. I'm not saying that I'm not important, but that's not where my main focus should be because at the same time this kid can't provide for himself. He can't feed himself. He can't change himself."

Me: How did the idea of being a father impact your everyday activities?

Chip: "I knew that I couldn't be out clubbin' until 4 in the morning on weekends because at the same time, somebody still has to care for him and he's not everybody else's child. I didn't like to put him off on people. You know it takes a village to raise a child, but that village didn't have him. So, I had to be more responsible for my actions. I had to make sure I was accountable. When somebody wanted to watch him or keep him I wasn't just going to put him on them all night. If you wanted to keep him for a couple hours while I took care of my business, if I gotta come back home with him, I gotta come home, that was that on that."

Me: What is the impact of the changes you made when you thought you were going to be a father, now that you are not the father of that child?

Chip: "It's crazy. It's a transition man. It's hard getting out of that. When people ask you to do something, and the only reason why you didn't was because you had to get to your child, it's like now will you? And now my focus is on my music and my passion and still overall being a better person. This situation, it just let me know that you can't take nothing for granted, nothing. You can't...

"I felt like being a father was truly a blessing, because I got a chance to do something that I was never taught to do, that I learned and I had to work at it. And that was something that I was willing to do... The goal was to be the best at it and I accomplished that cuz when I was there I did everything I had to do. So now my goal is to be the best at what I'm doing now. And I just gotta take that same effort and transfer it to something else, transfer learning. Just because it is a different situation doesn't mean it's a different tactic. So then it was being a father, now it's being a better musician or a better mentor or being just a better man in general, being not just a statistic, but a statistic that stands out. How can I elevate myself to get people to know that whatever I'm doing is always do my best?"

Me: Is there anything you want to add to your narrative?

Chip: "Just basically be careful. Everybody is not what they seem. You see something, but it's a lot deeper than that. I can smile now and be sad on the inside and you will never know it. So like a book, you can't judge it by its cover. You gotta read it, understand it, analyze it, take notes, and study it. Read it again to make sure you understand it. Nothing is what it seems. Everything takes work. So if it comes easy, you didn't want it."

My Reflection after Chip's Interview

My office (Memphis)

May 18, 2010. 3:05 p.m.

It hurt to see the pain on Chip's face as he reflected on the pain that came along with finding out the child he had raised for nearly two years was not his biological son. Chip had been a friendly, high-spirited person for as long as I had known him.

He couldn't have been older than 6 or 7 years old when we met. I didn't see much of Chip after I graduated high school in 1998. We reconnected via Facebook around 2008. I found out he was making a career of the saxophone and invited him to speak to students at the 2009 Lionel Linder Journalism Camp for *Teen Appeal*. I plan the city-wide high school newspaper's camp each year. The same friendly high-spirited Chip showed up with his saxophone and a small child whom he introduced as his son.

Chip played for the students at camp and impressed us all. He also invited me to come listen to him live. He only had to invite me to support him once before he had gained a fan. Half the reason I went was to hear the music and the other half was to support someone I had known since his early childhood. I've listened to Chip play his horn in several spots downtown and at other venues throughout the city. He was always smiling, always cheerful.

Today was the first time I can remember seeing hurt on his face and hearing it in his voice. I got the sense from him that he wanted to be that child's father. He said in the interview that he prayed that God would remove any doubts about the child's paternity.

The interview was successful. Chip gave heartfelt, in-depth responses to all the questions I had for him. I saw a couple sides of him I had never seen, though. I mentioned that I had never seen him express hurt the way he did during the interview, but that wasn't all. I hadn't ever seen him express such anger either.

I had never heard him use profanity before today, and we had been talking frequently since he came to my camp in August 2009. We discussed his music and future career plans as well as my writing and future plans. We talked a little about women and the different venues he had gigs at and other things. This is not to say that I was offended, because I was not. The young man had incredible reasons to be angry.

Listening to Chip's fresh story and the newness of his pain brought back memories of the pain and anguish I felt more than 10 years ago when I was a teenager struggling with my situation. I remember sitting on my parent's porch in Frayser looking out into the streets as rain dropped from the sky one evening. My dad pulled into the driveway and his first statement as he approached his teary-eyed son was, "Ain't no use in cryin' now. You did it now."

I had been watching it rain for quite some time by the time Pop pulled up. So many thoughts were running through my 18-year-old brain: How would I support a child? Would I still be able to go to college? What was I going to do? I was terrified.

I looked up at my dad and told him that I wore a condom when the girl and I had sex. "Every time" he asked. "We only did it one time," I answered. My dad told me right then and there that the child wasn't mine and that we were going to have a paternity test taken.

"We gettin' a test! And you can tell (her family) I said that!" he said.

I knew the chances of me being that child's father were slim, but I knew that condoms were not 100 percent effective too. And the girl was so convincing. She wrote in her diary about how she was hurt that I doubted her honesty. Her mother would sneak into her diary and call me to tell me about the sad journal entries her daughter had made.

I felt so guilty. I remember reasoning with myself: "You're hurting that girl and you're going to look like such a terrible father if the child is yours and you were not there for her mother during the pregnancy."

I shared that reasoning with my dad and he told me that I would have all the time I need to make up for it if the child turned out to be mine. I felt so weak, like all the life was being sucked from my body.

That experience took a part of me away. I remember holding that baby the day she was born. She was so precious and beautiful, so little. I almost believed I had created a little miracle, but in reality I had been lied to. I could see that pain freshly placed on young Chip's face. I felt his pain and mine all over again for a split second before regaining my composure.

Chapter 3
Entrepreneur

Eric's Briefing

My office (Memphis)

May 18, 2010. 5:25 p.m.

I'm excited about my interview with Eric today. He's a real talker so I expect him to hear some good quotes and for him to explain his experience in a clear, understandable way. Eric attended high school with my younger brother Gregory. I spent a significant amount of time with Eric while he was a high school student through his association with my brother.

Eric and a few of Greg's other friends would come over to my Memphis apartment to hang out with my brother. I was living in Raleigh Woods apartments when they started coming over to hang out. They would shoot pool in our living room, play darts, listen to music or watch movies. Eric was a year or two older than the other guys and it showed. He didn't joke around as much as the other teenagers. He was high-spirited and had fun with the guys, but he was the most mature and serious guy in the group.

Eric was a hustler too. He would do handy work, work on cars and take on other miscellaneous jobs for extra money. He was a business-minded fellow and didn't necessarily act like a kid.

I respected Eric's frank way of speaking when he was a youngster. He would speak his mind with the group of five or six that would frequent my crib. He didn't come across as shy or sneaky, but straight-forward. I probably esteemed that quality in him because it reminded me of my own personality.

I don't think I will change my approach a whole lot for Eric's interview. I feel like I did a good job of letting Chip do the talking during my interview with him earlier today and plan to do the same with Eric. I want him to share everything he has to say and I'm confident he will have a lot to say.

Eric's Interview

Me: Tell me about your relationship with the person who falsely said you were her child's father...

Eric: "It was a high school love. It started off in the seventh grade. Throughout high school we were on and off periodically through the years back and forth. Towards the ...about 11th grade we started to establish a real relationship and from that point on we continued a relationship even after high school. It was a high school love."

Me: How did y'all meet?

Eric: "Man, it was through a mutual friend. She said that she had somebody for me and I was just kind of intrigued by that, we met and kind of hit it off from there, although we are opposite of each other. We hit it off in like the seventh or eighth grade."

Me: What was the nature of your relationship?

Eric: "Like any practical boyfriend/girlfriend...You talking about during school or after?"

Me: Starting in high school...

Eric: "Just practical, casual dating. You know, and she [said] that I was one of the first boyfriend that she had ever had. So it was a big stepping stone for her. Just casual dating, man, you know kisses here, date there, hanging out, long phone calls, that typical high school thing."

Me: So what were your expectations for the relationship?

Eric: "Umm, I knew that she had class, man, even back then. She had a stable household. That was always something that I was attracted to, for longevity purposes anyway. I felt like my vision was to actually be with her at some point. That was my mind set at the time. This could really be my girlfriend for a while. So that was my projection on it."

Me: What kind of things did yall do? Tell me about a date.

Eric: "Umm man, at first she couldn't even....she had to sneak on the phone with me. That was middle school. Now going into high school a date was really like, sneaking over her house, mama coming home I'm right behind the door. You know, she laying there on the bed I'm sitting there, we smiling at each other while her mama talking to her. Me hiding in the closet one time when her mama came home. I had to run out of the house. One time and her daddy actually rode down on me and he was like, 'umm I don't like nobody in my house.' So that was a date for us. Man we didn't have no dates until she was like 16 or 17. She got a job and would come over my house after work and then we actually went to the prom together and umm you know that was like....well, we went to the movies a couple of time, but I don't think...I think we always had to sneak around and do it because her parents were so strict."

Me: For you, what kind of atmosphere did the relationship provide?

Eric: "Umm, a bit of stability for me at that point of life cuz I was definitely encountering a lot. Just that harmony, it was definitely a harmony there undoubtedly... She was very, very, umm, a bit submissive. She was infatuated with me literally; she would go that extra mile to please me. It was a great experience at all times, and I definitely took advantage of that at times. I definitely took advantage of that."

Me: What type of atmosphere do you think it created for her?

Eric: "Is that on the up side or the down side?"

Me: Both sides

Eric: "On the up side, me being one of those popular cats in school, I think that it definitely boosted her confidence, self-esteem, ummm … you know, just her as a person. I know on the up side it had to be the most beautiful thing. At times she used to tell me that she used to feel like she was the only woman there, the most important woman in the world. I just literally treated her like a queen, I really did. And that's the quote that sticks out to me the most. A lot of times when we were out she just felt like she was number one...like no one else was around.

"Now on the down side, man...just being that old playa, you know. Dealing with different ladies, her overhearing....dealing with the he-say-she-say, the propaganda that can come with being that popular guy she endured a lot of that. She withstood a lot of it cuz she kept coming back. She kept coming back, man. And I done her wrong, man, I must admit.

I took her down through there... I did... I really did. I kind of just played with her feelings."

Me: How?

Eric: "Umm, dealing with other young ladies...saying that we are official - we are one and not staying true to my word, making her look and feel foolish. Not just in her eyes but in her friend's eyes. You start to look foolish or just blatantly dumb...You know cuz love will do you like that. It doesn't matter at what level, if it's high school love or older love, you get it at the same capacity. It can make you be dumb, blind."

Me: That's what they say, everybody plays the fool sometimes, which leads me to my next question...how honest were you with her?

Eric: "Now during high school, I was not. After high school, I started to become real blunt actually and just telling her that no one meant anything but her. So at one point in time she knew that she was the other woman and she accepted that because she wanted to be in my presence, wanted to be with me whenever possible. So probably during the latter part I started to be honest, but not fully honest. I don't think at no point was just like 100%."

Me: At no point in the relationship were you 100?

Eric: "No, I don't think so. I've never... because that's the way I came up. Observing any man in my life, never kept it real...never...never ever. I never seen a man keep it 100. Always editing their words, always staying quiet, going with the flow. It is what it is. That's it. I never witnessed harmony in no man and woman relationship, never witnessed it...always overheard it, but I have never witnessed it."

Me: Was there ever a point when you said 'I'm going to keep it 100?'

Eric: "Oh yeah, towards the end. Towards the end, and that's bad man."

Me: What happened then?

Eric: "When I started to keep it 100? I think what ultimately happens when you start to tell the truth, the whole truth, is that you start to realize what will and will not change about a person or what compromises they will make in order to make a relationship prosper."

Me: Give me an example.

Eric: "Say for instance, you know as far as chemistry is concerned, day to day conversation wise, just acting off each other, being proactive or reactive. If I'm blunt about it and I tell her like, 'well I don't really like to talk with you, you know what I'm saying, cuz you always bringing this problematic approach or you evaluating or analyzing it too much and I'm not trying to go there.'

"Once you tell the whole truth instead of sitting back and being quiet, not saying nothing, I ain't finna talk to her, you giving all the negative vibes, but you not giving the negative feedback that you need to give in order to make it to the next level. Now the next level can be a more successful relationship or the next level can be the end, you know what I mean? When you keep it real, the real is on the floor. So either the next level is gonna be, you guys are trying to make this work, you trying to get to a point where you got more harmony between you all. If not, then the next step is the end, then you know. You really know the person. You really know what not to do cuz I just told you the real. But guess what? It's my first time telling you the real. All those other times I've just been sitting back not saying nothing cuz that's all I have ever seen. And I ain't even finna try to say nothing, cuz I don't think it's worth saying nothing."

Me: So, how did that affect your relationship?

Eric: "Man, look. Like it affects any other relationship I ever had… It's like I'm a bit optimistic, naturally. I have a very chipper personality. So anytime I am coming into a relationship I'm kind of eager. Know what I'm sayin'?

"(My outlook is) we gonna make it work, make it work. And then all of a sudden you aint meeting me half way, and now you not meeting me 40% and now you not meeting me 30% and now we down to 20, it's nothing, you know what I'm saying? Now you are down to nothing really. That's how it affects my relationship. All my eagerness, I guess it fills the void for that woman, you know what I mean? Sometimes I had to blame myself cuz I didn't let the woman step up like they should initially.

Me: I mean in this one specific relationship, not generally, in that one relationship. You decided to keep it 100, knowing where this may lead, how did that decision in that specific relationship, make a difference?

Eric: So, you asking, knowing that I kept it 100…..

Me: You said at no point did you keep it 100. Then you said there was a point when you wanted to. Later on you said you really, really wanted to, but you thought about the effect it could have. How did that affect you, just that thought process, being on that seesaw?

Eric: "How did it affect me? Not being 100, how did that affect me?"

Me: Yeah…

Eric: "Umm, it just beats you down man. I think that's all. It will just beat you down. You're not being you. You're not you."

Me: Outside of the giving you credit for a child that's not yours, how honest do you think she was with you?

Eric: "(deep breath…) I have to question all of that now, man. You know? For such a milestone like that to take place, I don't know. You question everything. After you experience that paternity it's like, I mean… Now if you still want me to give you an estimate of how, I mean…I think she was fairly honest with me. And then I don't know if she was fairly honest at all, ya know what I mean? Something like that for you to even try to go through…telling me I'm the father, you know what I mean?

Man that's treacherous! Know what I'm sayin'? That's diabolic! That ain't no joke!

Look, (laughing…..) I done told some lies, man, but look you finna put a lifetime lie on me…You know what I'm sayin'? I don't even know if I'm saying it the right way. You finna put a lifetime…lie…man. You know what I mean?…a lifetime sentence… I don't even want to say sentence, but you know. This is the real deal, no joke."

Me: Up until the point that you found out, from junior high, how honest did you think she had been with you?

Eric: "So honest. So honest, I never questioned anything about this young lady, do you hear me?…It's always been a question about me. I never doubted her, never ever. I really did not. And I have had girlfriends that I questioned. I never doubted this young lady, man."

Me: How often did you guys have unprotected sex?

Eric: "Well, I would say after 12th grade, we started picking up on the unprotected sex. Then after then it was just like… it was kind of on and off, man. Ummm, I would definitely say the ratio was 1:3 times that I would use a condom. One being the one time I used one; the other two I didn't."

Me: And this is…everyday…once a week….???

Eric: "This was a couple times a week, at least twice a week. That was for probably two or three years. Which makes it odd anyway, cuz I'm like, 'this is my baby. I've been in there raw so many times.'"

Me: Was there birth control being used?

Eric: "Supposedly… I can't quite…no… No, it wasn't. She had some things she disagreed with, side effects.

Me: So you all were willingly having unprotected sex, with no birth control a couple times a week?

Eric: "Right, cuz I…saw her as being my wife. This wasn't just a 'round the way girl.' She went through all this so, hey…"

Me: So what made you trust each other to that point?

Eric: I think things that we had…. Situations that we went through prior that had made us stronger. You know, or more tolerant. I said, 'Hey, we can persevere, we've seen the worst of the worst through high school, so we can get through it.' I think that mentally said to us both…'hey we've been through a lot, so we gonna make this work.'"

Me: At what point did you question the paternity of the child? The exact moment.

Eric: "The day he was born. You can ask my best friend cuz I turned around and told him. I said, 'Look. I don't know if I'm supposed to feel some type of genuine, authentic emotion right now in my heart, but I don't.' And I turned around and told him… 'I don't think this my child, man.' He looked at me and said, 'Yeah right… he's got your head.' I have a distinct head clearly, but genetics…whatever, whatever."

Me: What was the process once you got that feeling? What happened next?

Eric: "From that day on, I told my dad that I don't think that's my baby. He said 'yeah right boy whatever, you know that's your baby.'

"After that it was three months, man. And it kept pounding at me, pounding at me. You know what I'm saying? I put this on everything....I didn't have any type of speculation, no type of text messages, late phone calls, nothing along the lines of that to even give me an inkling that she slept with another man.

"So, I'm like, 'where is this coming from? Why do I keep thinking this?' So like three months passed and man it's stronger than ever at this point. I'm literally holding this child up beside me in the mirror at home.

"People may find that funny, but I don't man. It hurt. It hurt me bad to just even take my hands and put him up to my face. I'm like, 'naw, naw, naw. Why am I thinking this?'

"I'm hating myself for thinking like this. I hated myself.

"And it seemed like it gained more weight because I trust her and here he is. He has no idea about my thoughts and he doesn't deserve that, you know what I mean?

"It's a double effect for me...why, why am I thinking this? So three months passed and man I finally got enough courage to ask. And when I say it took a whole lot for me to ask, I guess the analogy would be like hollarin' at the first girl or something...whatever the hardest thing in your life would be...that's what it was.

"So, I said ummm...I said, 'I don't think this is my baby.'"

(Female): 'What? What you mean? You know I wouldn't do you like that! I can't believe you would say something like that! You know I love you!'

(Eric): 'You right, you right...I'm wrong, I'm stupid, I'm sorry. I don't know where this is coming from, I'm so sorry...I will never say that again, never do it again.'

"And I felt horrible once I did it. But man, it wasn't even 24 hours later, till it started pounding in my head again. I'm talking about this time it couldn't be nothing, but God. And I'm serious. It couldn't be nothing but God.

"I'm talkin' 'bout it started to pound on my head...boom, boom, boom. I'm like, 'don't think this Eric! I wanna be a daddy. He is my son.'

"I went to drive trucks for this family. I'm finna have a family. I'm gonna get married. I'm finna do the right thang. I'm finna take care of my kid.

"Six months down the road I took it upon myself to go ahead and act on my thoughts and got a paternity test.

"It was like 100 bucks through the internet. I ordered it. Swabbed his mouth, swabbed mine and I'm like breaking down at this point while I'm swabbing, you know what I'm saying? I felt so guilty. The whole time I'm anticipating the test results to come back, they finally come. The child is not yours….I'm like, 'okay it was 100 dollars, so that was a cheap test.'…(Eric and I are laughed,….)

"It's just 100, a cheap test very inaccurate lab probably ain't up to par….I called the lab. I say umm this can't be true. I called the lab. Do you hear me?…(Eric and I laughed).

I said something ain't right. Can this test be wrong? Them folks told me, 'No sir….there are no chromosomes matching.' (Eric and I laughed)

I'm talking bout I had so many feelings going through me at this time. I was down in New Orleans, naw I was down in Mississippi right around the time of Hurricane Katrina or six months past that.

Man, I'm down there. I got so many feelings going through me I am ready to beat, I'm ready to scream, I'm ready to smack myself upside the head.

I'm ready to give up at this time cuz I don't know what to do. I didn't know what to say or do. I called my dad and said, 'Dad you not gonna believe this.'

(Eric): The test results came back and that ain't my baby.'

(Eric's Dad) 'Son calm down. Calm down. Don't do nothing stupid.

(Eric) 'I'm finna come back home.'

I was ready to bash me some heads in around here. I was hot. Anyway I came back home. I went and got the 500 test from the (Memphis Radio Station) K97 dude. I'm at the K97 dude office, dude asked, 'can we take a picture'….can you take a picture?

Can you take a picture? You think this is a happy moment? Man I'm not takin' no picture. Wanna put me up on the board with the rest of the mamas and daddies. You know what I'm sayin'? You get a discount…. I ain't taking no damn picture, man I'm hurt.

I want this to be my kid. I mean I spent 550 with this man. The same results came back….Bam!

Boy, I rode ova to that house I bust up in that door. I asked her just like this.

(Eric): 'Who is the father of my son?'

(Female): 'What?'

(Eric): 'Who the father of my son?'

(Female): 'What you mean?'

And man, I threw them results at her, dawg. I threw them at her. And you ain't gone believe what she said then....

(Female) 'I got raped!'

(Eric): 'You got raped? For real?'

....I go all soft real quick... 'For real baby, what happened?'

Then click, click... 'Hell naw, you ain't been raped. You ain't tell me nothing about it? Nothing?...You didn't tell yo mama? Nobody? Nothing?'

(Female): 'It happened in the back of the car we were coming home one night from the club....he knew he took advantage of me. Somebody I knew from when we were younger.'

... There it is right there, as soon as she said that.

(Eric): You knew him and you didn't tell nobody?...Cut throat....She started screaming.

(Female) 'What about me? What about me?'

(Eric) 'What about you? What about me bitch?'

So that was the conclusion of that.

Now let me tell you what the real scenario was... My daddy wasn't in my life. My step-dad was in my life, my whole life since I was about one year old, so I know the power of a step-father.

Dawg, if she woulda told me... I probably...I'm more then 98% sure I woulda been in (the child's) life. I would have been daddy...a fulltime daddy. Cuz I know the power of a step-daddy. Only if she had been honest, I would have had no problem taking care of that child.

Now this is the transition I really had to go through because I was driving trucks and there is nothing but isolation anyway and you don't have time to do nothing but think, right?

So at the time I said, 'we gonna make the relationship work anyway.' I tried to work it out with her anyway, so we get back into the relationship.

I'm trying to make it work cuz one thing I don't want is a fatherless child and then again I know how a step-father can impact a life. But my heart grew colder and colder man until it just turned into an ice brick. And that was it... it was over. It was over."

Me: You mentioned that she knew who the father was. Did she let him know that he was the child's father?

Eric: Yeah..... As soon as I found out I wasn't she contacted him and got the test and sure enough, he was the father. And he actually stepped up. I knew him too. That's the ironic part about it.

Me: How did you finding out you were not the father impact your sense of self?

Eric: "Well, I mean for me, what it did was lower my trust for the human race. It's not even... I'm not pointing at women because I went through so much coming up. But what you say? What did it do for self?"

Me: How did you feel about yourself?

Eric: "I felt...I felt worthless."

Me: Why?

Eric: "Knowing I had all of the right intentions and I was taking actions on those intentions. I really went to drive trucks. I felt worthless, like I was used."

Me: How did that experience affect your view of women, dating and of sex?

Eric: "Now, I'ma tell you one thing. I guess it's a side note. I was really good at pulling out... (laughing...) you know what I mean?

"Unfortunately all those years she didn't get pregnant and when she did get pregnant, she wasn't pregnant by me. Maybe that's crazy for me to think that way, but that's just how I thought about it at one point in time.

"Anyway, women, man lord have mercy. It went downhill, the trust factor. Still to this day I'm skeptical of any and everything, as far as marriage, as far as trust, as far as just day to day, sexually wise. I feel more prominent about abstinence cuz that will take you away from the whole equation period. That's the ultimate solution no matter how you look at it. Not the protected or unprotected part...just abstinence. Sex is not sacred like you think it is...it's just a hobby, and some people love to do it."

Me: So you felt differently before that experience? About sex?

Eric: "Oh yeah, I felt that it was sacred, it's a bond… umm, you know. I'm not gonna sit here and say that I have not had a one-night stand or casual sex, but mentally I always felt strong about sexual relations. I really have, I really have. And I think I kind of compare that to some of the other guys I know….that it's just like something to do…bam, bam from the rooter to the tooter and you gone. Any sexual partner I have ever had, we had a good repartee with each other. You know what I mean?….yeah… yeah so…"

Me: What stands out in your mind as the most valuable experience that you will take away from this?

Eric: "Follow your heart. That is the most valuable. I'm able to forgive and forget. I'm able to still do whatever. But man, follow your heart. Cuz that's all I had.

"Again, I honestly did not have any type of evidence…no email, no text, no nothing to… not even late nights or whatever. And I followed my heart, man. That's it. The end. I went off my intuition …Follow your heart."

Me: What type of changes did you make when you thought you were going to be a father?

Eric: "I was in college at the time. I said, 'I'm not about to struggle. I'm about to go out here and get me a skill' and I chose truck driving. I started driving trucks man, in order to prepare financially to do what I had to do to be a father and a husband. That's exactly what I did."

Me: You made that change, how did that play out once you were no longer looking at yourself as a father?

Eric: "Once I did find out it was a bit of depression as the aftermath that occurred with me personally. Umm, it was just long days, long weeks. This was the very reason that I went on the road, because of this child, because of this family, in order for my family to be in a better place. But that was stage one, after that…

"I couldn't do the road any more simply because I couldn't let that eat away at me man… that thought….cuz that's all you have time to do. After that man, the most important, one of the pinnacle moments in my life happened. I started my business. Being an entrepreneur, that was always one of my dreams."

Me: Why do you say your business came out of that?

Eric: "I say that cuz I couldn't do the truck driving anymore simply because I couldn't think of that anymore and I had to make a transition into another occupation. So with the capital that I saved to make the family thing happen, I took that same capitol and invested in my business. That very money I was gonna make that family with, I put into the business."

Me: And how long ago was that?

Eric: "That was almost three and a half years ago."

Me: And how is the business now?

Eric: "Aw man, business is good. Business is unbelievable. (Deep breath) It's a dream come true. And I'ma leave it at that…It's really a dream come true."

Me: additional comments:

Eric: "I have a friend, one of my best friends that says, 'Good guys always finish last.'

Good guys finish last in man's eyes. Good guys finish first in God's eyes. Because if you are doing what you need to do, then that's the only eyes you need to be concerned about. I guess I can go as far to say that I was a good guy to some extent.

And man just take…appreciate who you are and what you are about and focus on self and everything else will fall into place.

For a long time I was reactive to whom I'm dealing with…whether it's a woman, friendship or family member and I took it upon myself to be proactive.

And I think that the pro-activeness generated my intuition, my heart, and that's what I followed in this situation and I came out on top. And that's what I have been following ever since. And here is another testimony in my business and I just keep following my heart. That's what I took from this whole situation."

My Reflection after Eric's Interview

My office (Memphis)

May 19, 2010. 2:35 p.m.

Eric's interview went as well as I expected. He was straight-forward and honest. I was somewhat surprised he didn't get emotional. He had done so in past conversations about the situation. I guess the healing process has helped with time. It has been approximately three years since he found out the child he thought was his son was not.

His only concern about participating in the interview was the emotional welfare of the child. He said he did not want the child to be upset about the story. I told him I would not use the child or mother's name in the narrative to secure their privacy. I cannot impress to my friends, interview participants and readers enough that this project is aimed at understanding the experiences of the men involved and not passing judgment on them or the women they were in relationships with.

Eric was explicit about discussing the mistakes he made in the relationship. He admitted to lying to his ex-girlfriend and having sex with other women after telling her that he would be faithful to her. Although he made attempts to justify his infidelity to his girlfriend by mentioning that all the men he knew were unfaithful, he still took full responsibility for his actions.

I expected him to say that that her sleeping with another man might have been karma or payback, but he never said anything like that. I'm not implying that her infidelity was karma or payback either, but I know people often think that way. I once thought that I should never remarry after my divorce because I had cheated on my ex-wife and would later be cheated on in some act of karma if I were to remarry. I shared my thoughts with my older brother and he told me that payback comes in many forms and that the wrongdoer often doesn't choose his retribution or know what it will be. At any rate, Eric never mentioned his ex-girlfriend lying to him being a case of 'what goes around comes around.'

I was pleased to see a lot of the bitterness he once carried in his heart had seemingly gone away, or at least lessened. I can't help to think back to young Chip whose situation is still so fresh. I remember when Eric looked as sad and hurt when discussing his situation as Chip did when we talked yesterday. I guess the bright side is that time will heal his wound as well. I remember when I was all torn up more than a decade ago myself.

I sincerely hope these narratives benefit individuals and families and serve as therapy for families and individuals who need it. This is not about digging up old dead bones to talk about how stinky they smell, but rather to share experiences so others who might be dealing with similar situations can heal better.

Chapter 4
Pimp

Dre's Briefing

May 21, 2010. 5:49 p.m.

Nashville. Dre's apartment

I rode into Nashville with Randy, one of Dre's frat brothers. We met on several occasions and were both groomsmen in Dre's wedding. Randy and I discussed the concept for this book on the way here. He was impressed and said he looked forward to reading the finished product.

I look forward to hearing Dre's narrative because I've never heard the whole story. I was riding through Frayser, the neighborhood where we both grew up in Memphis, and I saw Dre's car in his parents' driveway. He was visiting home from college.

I hugged his parents and we started talking about old times. Dre introduced me to a young lady and a child I had never seen before. He said the female was his girlfriend and the child was his daughter. He had heard through the hood that I had a daughter of my own and asked how the baby was doing. From there, I told the story of how I got a paternity test that revealed I was not the child's father. I told the story in front of Dre, his parents and the girl and child that were there.

I never thought twice about the conversation after leaving Dre's house. It had been nearly a year since I had seen my first best friend in life and I was happy to see him and his parents.

Dre and I lived in the same neighborhood in the '80s and '90s. My mother was strict and Dre's house was one of the few places I could go to play. When Dre's father asked me to do something I listened to the instruction like I was coming from my own father. When his mom spoke it was just like listening to my mom.

It was another year or so before I saw Dre again after that visit years ago. When I talked to him next, he told me the child I met was not his daughter. I'm excited about hearing the details today.

Dre's Interview

Me: Tell me about the relationship with the person that falsely said that you were her child's father...

Dre: "Our relationship started off good; I met her at a night club. Me and some friends were hanging out, she and her friends were hanging out. She was looking cute. I know I was looking good. She was a little older than me. She had already graduated from high school and I was a junior or senior in high school, probably a senior. It was early in the year. I vaguely remember, but long story short, we ended up getting together and having a relationship."

Me: What was the nature of the relationship with her? Was it casual dating, were y'all boyfriend/girlfriend?

Dre: "A little bit of both. We were casually dating, boyfriend/girlfriend. She was an older chick, she was spoiling me. She used to set me out, take me to the mall, buy me new shoes and she had a nice car and her own apartment. I had a relationship, a real relationship, with a high school sweetheart that she tarnished."

Me: Ok, what were your expectations for the relationship?

Dre: "I had no expectations. I was just young, dumb and fulla cum actually. Ya know, light skinned older lady, pretty eyes, pretty hair...you know I was just...just young dumb and fulla cum to be honest man and umm. I remember during sex, I vaguely remember that, it just popped up in my head that.....I remember she said she had surgery or something in the past and she had told me that she couldn't have babies, something dealing with her sex. So me being young and we were having sex anytime I wanted it, I didn't use condoms on a couple of occasions."

Me: What do you think her expectations were for the relationship?

Dre: "I think she knew where I was headed. She knew my mind set. She knew I was gonna be a successful young man, so she was looking at it as a jackpot... a winning situation for her."

Me: Tell me about one time you remember y'all hanging out...

Dre: "Going the movies, running around. Celebration Station was open around that time…running around celebration station, riding go karts, all types of shit, just typical dating."

Me: *So, what kind of atmosphere did the relationship provide for you?*

Dre: "Like I said, I was a young guy, so it provided an atmosphere like I finally got an older chick that is going to trick off some money to me. So it provided me like… damn near like I was a pimp. You know, I could receive money on demand, shoes on demand, clothes on demand and not to mention at the time I was a freshman in college. I didn't have a car my first couple months of class. And she came down every weekend to get me, bring me back to Memphis, take me back to (my out of town campus) and she would drive back to Memphis every weekend. She was doing all this stuff."

Me: *How many years older than you was she?*

Dre: "I'ma say about four or five years older than me."

Me: *So, if you were 17 when yall met she was about 21?*

Dre: "Yeah."

Me: *What kind of atmosphere do you think the relationship provided for her?*

Dre: "She had a young brother that knew what he wanted. Self driven, self motivated and was determined for success."

Me: *How honest were you with her?*

Dre: "I was honest with her. I introduced her to my family and I met her family. I didn't hide anything from her… She knew I had other females that were my age. She didn't care, she just wanted me."

Me: *Now, excluding the paternity incident, how honest do you think she was with you?*

Dre: "As far as I saw, she was cool. She was kind-hearted. She wasn't a bad person. She wasn't trifling up until that point, if you ask me. She took care of business for the little girl. She wasn't a bad mama. You know ummm, she handled her business."

Me: *What made you comfortable enough to have unprotected sex?*

Dre: "After being with each other a long time, I probably didn't have a condom or access to one... once we were getting started to have sex... That's a good question... I don't know what made me comfortable enough to have sex with her without a rubber. Thinking back on it now, on how serious the issue is now and me being like a high school student then, I wasn't worried about getting no disease and this and that....I just can't say, I can't say."

Me: *So how often did you all have unprotected sex?*

Dre: "Not that much, not that much. Out of the 5 times we did it, I give it once."

Me: *So 1 out of 5...and this is over the course of the two years?*

Dre: "Yeah."

Me: *Okay. What made you believe you were the father of the child?*

Dre: "Cuz like I said, I thought she was an innocent little quiet girl and I knew I had unprotected sex with her and I knew I had ejaculated in her. I was just trying to do the right thing: accept my responsibility."

Me: *What was your reaction when you found out that she was pregnant?*

Dre: "Well, she told me. And I remember saying, 'oh okay. You're pregnant?' She said, 'Yeah and you the daddy.'

It wasn't a happy reaction and it wasn't a sad reaction, it was just, 'you the daddy.'"

Me: *What kind of adjustments did you make once you find out you were becoming a father?*

Dre: "Once I found out I was about to become a father it kinda made me step my game up a little bit. It made me start hustling, taking chances on getting kicked out of school... tryna get money. I didn't have a job in college, you know...so I was hustling man, it was class and hustling."

Me: What made you question the paternity of the child?

Dre: "As I got more distanced away from her and just cut her off, stopped messin' with her, she started doing more cruel stuff. A couple females, cuz I used to have little girls with me all the time…a couple females had mentioned it…they were like, 'that is not your baby. That baby don't look nothing like you.'"

"I was in denial, but the thing that made me…I was gonna do it. I was gonna get a blood test anyway. I wasn't there when the baby was born. I said I was gonna get a blood test. I just didn't want to say the baby wasn't mine and then it came out mine. I didn't want to be in that type of category.

"The baby came early. It was premature and I wasn't there. I was in college and came home. The baby was in the hospital and you know she was sitting there with the baby in the baby bed and we kinda took it from there.

"I took my grandmother with me and asked her what she thought. She said, 'That's your baby.'… Of course, both of us light-skinned and the baby was pretty, so it could be a possibility. As time went on, I was only coming home on weekends and holidays. The baby started getting older, saying 'daddy.' You know umm…knowing me as daddy… crying when I left and all that type of stuff.'

"But the ultimate decision was, my sister was on Shelby county jail .com where you can plug in your information, anybody's information, and tell if they have any warrants out for them. Anything you want to get as far as Shelby County, and my name popped up. She called me while I was at work. She said, 'Do you know you got a warrant out for your arrest?' … She told me 'You got a paternity warrant.'

"I told you I never signed the birth certificate, cuz I wasn't there when she was born so she had a paternity warrant out for my arrest. I set up time to come home from school and turned myself in. I didn't have to go to jail. They let me go on what they call a field release cuz I willingly turned myself in. My dad went down there with me.

"My dad said, 'How much is a blood test,' to the lady who was processing my paper work. She said '$135.00.' My dad said, 'Shit, give him two of 'em (Dre and I laughed…).' So that was the ultimate decision."

Me: What was your reaction when you found out that you were not the father of the child?

Dre: "Hot! I was mad, disappointed, disgusted. I felt had...."

Me: Take me back to that day. As much as you can remember about getting the results....

Dre: "Man, me and my (fraternity brother) had came down, me and Nate came down from (my college). We were talking about it all the way down. I was like, 'man the closer we get to this point, I really think it's a strong possibility that this is not my child.

'You know, I could be wrong, but I just got this feeling now.' So we talking and talking and talking and she's calling me saying umm..... 'so, the blood test tomorrow,' I was like 'yeah.'

"I asked her, 'what you think about it?'

"She said, 'I don't think nothing about it. I think you gonna be paying that money...that fee.'

" If the baby was mine I had to pay a fee and if it wasn't she had to pay. So I said, 'aw that's cool.'

"She was like, 'but umm (the baby) needs umm $200.00 to do something. Can you get that to me?'

"And the way she said it kinda of struck a nerve. You know it kinda struck a nerve wit' me. So I was like, 'naw I ain't goin'...I'm not goin'...I'm gone wait until after this blood test before I give you any more money.'

"Then she went off...I forgot her exact words, but it ticked her off.... she said, 'you gone be sad cuz this yo baby.'

"I told her, 'aite, bet,' and we hung up the phone.

"The next morning my daddy cooked breakfast and mom was at work. We were sittin' up eatin'. I said well I'm getting ready to go on down to the courthouse.

"Nate said, 'well, I'm gone stay here and mess wit' ya daddy.'

"Nate stayed at the house wit' my dad, so I went to the courthouse myself.

"I walked in there, the courtroom and um I saw one of my friends I went to high school with...he was like, 'you gettin' ready to be put on child support too?'

"I was like 'yeah, but I want to make sure this baby is mine.'

"He was like, 'shid... me too.'

"So all these people were coming in, it was a packed day. So you got all these people coming up and they are saying umm, 'you are 99% the father, you are 98.7% the father.'

"Then my friend's baby momma comes up and I tell him… 'yo baby momma is as fine as hell.'

"He said, 'yeah she is ain't it?' Then we started laughin' about that. I said, 'dawg, you know that's your son, he look just like you.'

"He was like, 'shid… well if the test say it ain't…then it ain't (laughing…).' So um, that was pretty funny.

"Then my baby momma came in and she sat in the back, well ex-baby momma. I will never forget the order that they were calling the names. They would say the woman vs. the man. By the way my friend was 99% the father of his child (laughing…..). But when they called my case they said me vs. her.

Me: Cuz you initiated the case….

Dre: "Okay, could be… so I get up there and we standing in front of the judge. I'm on the left and she on the right. She had the baby in her hands. The results came back and (said plaintiff) is not the biological father of (said child).

"So I kinda turned around like that (demonstrates head turn), and looked at her out the corner of my eye like I was gone grab her. Know what I'm talkin' 'bout? But she ran over there with the clerk like she was in shock.

"But when the judge saw that he was like, '(sir) you can go.'

"So I walked outta there, dawg. I was upset…yeah I was angry. She was embarrassed. She ran out callin' my name and I stopped in the middle of the street.

"She said 'I'm sorry,' She apologized. She said, 'I am sooo sorry.'

"I just walked off.

"The baby was crying. I never heard that little girl cry like that. But from that point on I just let everything go. I let everything go.

"The first person I called was her mother. Her mother and I used to get into it all the time, she would try to tell me I was wrong cuz I stopped messin' with her daughter.

"I said, 'I hope you and your daughter burn in hell.'

"She was like 'what, what?'

"I said, 'you heard me. That ain't my motherfuckin' child!'

"She said, 'oh lord. You lying.'

"I said, 'that is not my got damned child. Call your daughter,' and hung-up the phone.

"I went to the house. Nate and my dad were having a pretty good little conversation. I told them it wasn't my baby. I was upset. Me and Nate kicked it, went to the bar, got me a 5th of that (Hennessey) and started drankin'.

"Pops went to work... just me and Nate there. Mom came home, she knew about it. She was more hurt than I was cuz she was a grandparent and she liked the little girl. We were drankin' and mom said, 'that bottle aint gonna make that baby yours.'

"I was like, 'yeah but its gonna help me out for right now.'

Me: You said a few time that you were angry, hot, upset, why?

Dre: "Because I felt like I was robbed. I was robbed of something. I felt like that was my blood line. When you get attached to something it's different. You got a little girl that's calling you daddy. I mean you have changed her diapers, you kissin' her, you nurturin' her. Know what I'm talkin' bout?....You a daddy. That's how I was hurt, upset. That's just like somebody coming to you telling you that something happened to your child.....you would be upset too, anybody would who is human."

Me: So how did this affect your view of women, dating and of sex?

Dre: "Oh man I turned into a...but I was...I was bitter, I was bitter. It really turned me into a ...it really stepped my game up.

"It made me stronger as far as dealing with relationships and women. No longer did I want a relationship. Every female was my friend. That was it. I was disrespecting females more than ever. I just didn't want a relationship with them.

"'If I'm messing with you, it's open. If I'm messing with her, it's open and don't say anything to me about it cuz I don't give a damn about you.' Once that process was over, my next girlfriend was my wife. I had no girlfriend after that.

"Not to mention, two weeks before that, I had a relationship with a female at Jackson State and she had gotten pregnant by me. And I was like, 'I don't want two different babies by two different baby mommas, especially while this court case was pending.'

"I thought that this baby could be mine...it was a fifty/fifty chance. So she had an abortion a week before I found out that this baby wasn't mine. And that was a good relationship that possibly could have ended up on the next level. But I lost her and that baby in like back to back weeks.

I was bitter. I was bitter. I was slayin (having strictly sexual relationships) em everyday if I wanted 'em. My next girlfriend became my wife."

Me: You said earlier that you didn't have money. You started hustling to have money for your family, when you found out that this wasn't your child, how did that affect your hustler mentality?

Dre: "It didn't. It stayed there cuz I was hungry. I always have been hungry. I've never been content. But by me having a child it made me more aggressive. Made me more aware of what I needed to do to provide because....it's hard to explain if you aint got no kids, how you want to provide and do for them...It's hard to explain. You gotta do what you gotta do."

Me: What do you think is the most valuable lesson that you learned?

Dre: "Never listen to a female when she says she can't have babies, always protect you and when in doubt always get a paternity test regardless of how it affects that female. Don't worry about losing a relationship with her, just go ahead and do it."

Me: What do you think men and women can do to prevent these situations?

Dre: Men can use protection, rubbers, condoms. That's about it. And women just need to know who they're sleeping wit'. They gonna do what they wanna do just like a man is, but I think they just oughta know.... 'On this date I had sex with him and on this date I had sex with him'.... for their own records so they will be 100% right, so they won't put nobody else in that bind.

Me: Do you have any additional comments......

Dre: I think we pretty much covered everything. Just for these people who are in doubt, if you are in doubt and you got a baby and you dark-skinned and your wife or girl is dark-skinned and the baby comes out light-skinned... go and get that test. Ya know what I'm talkin' 'bout. You should be able to see some characteristics of you in the baby. The signs are there, don't avoid no signs. Don't avoid any signs.

My Reflection after Dre's Interview

My office (Memphis)

May 27, 2010. 1:17 p.m.

I had a great time hanging out in Nashville with Dre. We talked and laughed about old times and memories and made some new memories. I didn't know what to expect from Dre on the interview because I had never heard his story. All I knew was that he introduced a female to me as the mother of his daughter, then a year or two later he told me that the child was not his after all.

Dre has one of the best all-around personalities I've ever seen. He gets along with everybody. Most people I know, even those with great personalities, often have groups of people or types of people they would rather not interact with, but Dre isn't like that. I don't know what should get credit for that aside from his parents doing a good job raising him and him gaining exposure to different environments and types of people at an early age.

I was curious as to what his feelings toward the female who falsely accused him of paternity would be like. Would he hate her? Want to hurt her? I was curious.

I would have to say the reactions and stories I got from Dre last weekend were pretty consistent with the Dre I knew as a child and reconnected with as an adult. He played it cool when the female said she was pregnant. He knew there was a high likelihood that he was the father and he shouldered the situation practically and honestly. I always appreciated the practical nature of Dre's family when I was a child. They were some of the most down-to-earth people I knew. No fakeness, no high horses, no facades, just real people. Those characteristics were special to me because my parents grew up on farms. I liked Dre's family because they reminded me of the down-to-earth everyday people in my family.

I noticed different habits and priorities among many of the city dwellers in Memphis as oppose to the priorities of my country family in Tipton County. The country folk spoke more broken English whereas the people in the city paid more attention to grammar. The city dwellers were more concerned with ambition and progression whereas the country folk were primarily concerned with family and contentment. City dwellers seemed to view material possessions of high importance whereas country folk esteemed quality time. It seemed as if I lived in two different worlds.

One world was in the hood, North Memphis, Frayser. Many of my classmates lived in housing projects and came from single-parent homes. Tipton County, where my parents grew up, was another world. My paternal grandfather owned pigs and chickens. Also, men usually married the women they impregnated (e.g. my father and mother). Strangely enough, I loved both worlds, but felt like an outsider in both worlds at the same time.

I never felt like one world was better than the other. They were just different. One fast-paced and busy, the other laid back and relaxed. I felt like an outsider because I didn't totally belong to either world.

Spending time with my family in Tipton County on weekends and summers was fun and free. I always knew I was safe. I could smile, dance and be myself. It was pure, simple love. Going to school and interacting in my neighborhood was challenging at times. Many of my classmates weren't as free-spirited as me. There were fights and cursing matches and students would make fun of those who couldn't afford brand name shoes and clothes.

My friendship with Dre was different, though. We never made fun of each other. We rode our big wheels together, and then we graduated to bikes. We played football, basketball and video games. He ate at my house and I ate at his house. He was family, not just a best friend.

I'm an extrovert in that I speak out when necessary and I can communicate with people of all sorts. I might not befriend them, though. I talk to doctors, teachers, administrators, students and executives with regularity in my line of work, but they are not all necessarily my friends. I am an introvert in regards to friendship. I don't have a large database of people I call to hang out or talk about my day. Dre was my first best friend.

I had another best-friend after Dre. The other best friend is currently incarcerated. Neither of those guys was major players in my life around age 16. Dre had transferred to another high school on the other side of town. My other friend was spending time with guys who I didn't share as much in common with me as he and I shared. This was around the same time my brother, Marland, was murdered.

I became more critical of people and didn't want to get close to anyone for a while after losing three people so close to me. I built a shell of words around me and used writing as my best-friend and therapy. I saw Dre from time to time if I rode through Frayser and saw his car at his parents' house.

We finally reconnected around 2006 or 07. He had graduated college and bought a house in the old neighborhood. I really didn't know what to expect from him because it had been more than a decade since we were running buddies. Over time, I came to realize that my childhood friend had not changed one bit. He was simply more educated and mature. I was proud of him.

We played dominoes, drank Hennessey, went to a few night clubs, barbecued and hung out. I was a groomsman in his wedding. Still, we were adults leading busy lives so there were a lot of conversations we never held. The issue of paternity from the 90s was one such conversation. I was impressed with the interview. He was blunt and straight-forward, as he had always been.

Dre told his story in a clean, detached manner. His paternity case was settled nearly a decade ago, which I believe allowed him to express himself with less emotion than Chip, who was very emotional after received his test results within months of my interviewing him. Although Dre said he was hot and upset when he got his paternity test results, he was less dramatic than Eric as well. It seemed to truly be a case of time healing old wounds.

He mentioned that the girl who falsely accused him was a good person when they dated and a good mother when the child was born. I was surprised by the frequency with which he and the girl had unprotected sex. He said he thought she was an innocent, quiet girl, which apparently was all he needed to know in order to have unprotected sex with her.

I was also surprised by how bitter Dre said he became. I never knew him to be a vengeful or spiteful person. He was one of the nicest and friendliest people I knew growing up. I could relate, though. I was bitter following my paternity test results, too. It seems to be somewhat of a natural inclination to lash out when you feel like you've been wronged. Both Dre and I lashed out by sleeping with different women on a regular basis.

Chapter 5
Hit It & Quit It

Big Tee's Briefing

My home (Memphis)

May 28, 1:18 p.m.

I look forward to listening to Big Tee tell his story. He's a humble, soft-spoken guy but is straight-forward and poignant at the same time. He has toned down a great deal since we were teenagers. He was once a bully, but now he is one of the nicest and most generous people I know. I wonder how much his paternity experience has to do with his change in his temperament.

Big Tee was adamant about keeping confidentiality to respect his wife's privacy. Therefore I won't delve too far into specifics about my relationship with him in order not to compromise his family's privacy.

Big Tee's Interview

Me: Tell me about your relationship with the person who falsely said you were her child's father...

Big Tee: "She is actually the mother of my first child."

Me: How did you two meet?

Big Tee: "We actually worked together for about two years. One thing led to another. We started dating a little bit and um, after she was pregnant with my daughter we broke up. And from there, after my daughter was born we... like I said we discontinued the relationship once she was pregnant with my daughter and we hadn't dealt with each other, hadn't been friends or nothing like that. We just had to deal with one another for the child.

Me: Ok, so how many children did she have?

Big Tee: "She had two before my daughter."

Me: Did those two children have the same father?

Big Tee: "Yes."

Me: How many children do you have?

Big Tee: "I have two....one by her and I just recently had a baby. She is 6 months old."

Me: Congratulations. What was the nature of your relationship with your oldest child's mother?

Big Tee: "Well, we started out dating, exclusively just me and her. Then I found out she had some type of relationship with her other baby's father, so we broke it off. That was initially why we broke it off.

"She called me... maybe a month later, after I guess she didn't like the ways things were going with him or he didn't like the way things were going with her. One way or the other she was just asking, you know, should we get back together. By that time, it was no. 'No way, I'm not messing with you. I don't want to deal with you.'

"So then she says, 'okay. Can we just still kick it? Can we still just mess off for a while?'

"Now, a light bulb goes on in my head and says, 'Mane, don't do it.'

"But the other side of me said 'Man, she was a good piece of tail. Go ahead and keep hittin' it from time to time.'

"So I kept hittin' it from time to time. By that time I got bored or uninterested because it wasn't the same. I was just like, 'Man we done.'

"And that's when she says, 'I'm pregnant.'

"So, I'm like, 'what….for real? You really mean to tell me that you are pregnant.'

"Come to find out she was pregnant. I didn't believe it was mine. I didn't believe my first daughter was mine because we weren't together, but we went and had the paternity test and to make a long story short she was mine.

"A couple years later, like I said, our relationship after my daughter was born was simple…I would come and pick her up at this time, I pay her bills, I take care of her like that. That was our relationship. No sexual relationship. We weren't friends. We weren't kickin' it, nothing.

"So, one day…one night she caught me slippin.' She called me up and said, 'hey. Do you mind stopping by here?'

"It was like (midnight).

"I'm like, 'it's 12 at night. If I come by there you know what I'm coming for and I don't deal with you like that.'

"She asked me anyway. I said, 'no.'

"The next night she called, same situation, the same scenario around the same time.

"I was like, 'why not? Just to see what it was like again.'

"So I went. I did the business and umm… Maybe, we can just go back to business as usual. I mean it was just that one time. Back to strictly about my baby…no friends no kickin' it, nothing like that.

"So three or four months later she hit me up... 'I'm pregnant.'

"My response to her is…. 'So what, why you tellin' me? Congratulations.'

"She tried to convince me then that her new baby was mine. I didn't wanna hear it, but I knew that she was fertile because she already had two before me, my daughter being her third child. I know that she is fertile.

"We started off using protection and I took it off, so there was a chance that it could have been mine.

"So time goes on and the baby comes. So now she's like, 'I know you gonna step up to the plate and do what you supposed to do.'

"I'm just like, 'that baby ain't mine.'

"She said, 'whatever. This baby is yours.'

"She took the baby by my folks' house. My mom was just like… 'yeah that's your baby.'

"I'm still saying that's not my baby. I was playing…at that time the song came out "That Baby Don't Look Like Me"…and it was really tripping me out cuz I'm really not wanting this to be my child because I remember what happened with my first daughter and how many problems we were having and how she kinda made life a little hectic at times. It was something I just didn't want. I didn't want to deal with her like that again.

"So, she's telling friends, family, (people at) the daycare where my daughter goes…anybody that will listen, 'this is (my) baby.'

"Finally, like eight to nine months later after the baby has been here, because I hadn't been a part of the baby's life, it finally kinda wore on me cuz my daughter and the new baby went to the same daycare. The people at the daycare center…man I could just feel the ugly looks like, 'man. How can you care so much about the first one and you don't even acknowledge the existence of the second one?'

"So I finally was like, 'I tell you what, you say this is my daughter. I may not like it and I may not like you, but if I did this then I have to go ahead and step up to the plate. Let me go ahead and get her one day.'

"So I went to pick her up from daycare and I actually had this paternity test that I ordered on-line from a website and I took the test and waited for the results. Well, the results came back maybe six weeks later. Naw, it wasn't that long, some weeks later. I'm not really sure how long, but when the results came back…the baby wasn't mine and of course I'm excited.

"All I remembered was that song she would sing… 'I'ma take you to court, I'ma take you to court.'

"And my thing is, once I found out the results, I was like, 'cool. I know the baby is not mine go ahead and take me to court.'

"Now once I found out the baby wasn't mine I told my mom and my family. Outside my family I pretty much hadn't told anyone. I was just like, 'I don't care what anyone else thinks. I know the baby is not mine.'

"We were playing basketball one day at the gym. We play on Saturdays and I actually told one of my homeboys and he just kinda broadcasted it to everybody. The guys that we play basketball with are the same guys we been playing with for years.

"So like a week later, she just pops up over my house and was just like, 'why do you have people in our business?'

"I was like, 'what?'

"She said, 'I heard you took a test and found out that the baby is not yours.'

"I said, 'yeah, so, and what? That baby ain't mine, you tried to plant a baby on me, she wasn't mine… Now you have to go find somebody else.'

"So I guess what really tripped me out about her response to it was… she didn't have a response of guilt or feeling bad that she tried to put this baby on me. Her whole thing was I found out and didn't tell her…so I dunno."

Me: You said you found out that she was cheating when y'all were actually a couple, how did you find that out?

Big Tee: "I found out that she was cheating because one of her neighbors was just like… you know I came by her house… I had a key to her apartment, so I used to come by the apartment whenever I wanted to. One day she wasn't there and I didn't think anything about it. The neighbor said she left with another dude in a car. So that's when I was like, 'oh for real?'

"So I was like, 'aw okay, and umm that's how I found out about that.'

"It was like that first baby daddy thing and she tried to play it off like….saying that he had to take her to the doctor or something because she didn't have a car, but I wasn't buying that so…we just split."

Me: You said after that it wasn't the same?

Big Tee: "After that we broke up. I'm not sure if that incident… that's what was on my mind. I remember saying that's it. But then you know, she's crying tears, crying tears so I'm like, 'aite cool.'

"A week later that's when she called me up to break up with me about him. So now that I'm thinking about it, that's what happened.

"She called me a week later to break up saying, 'I'm sure you gonna be happy…'

"I'm like, 'oh. You really don't have to sing this song…if you trying to move on go ahead I'll holla at ya. You and him be happy.'

"She called me back, like I said, because somebody wasn't happy.

"'So now you want to come back to me?' I'm not hearing it at that time cuz its just like you done hit a man's pride. You don't break up with me then try to holla back at me. So that's when she called asking if we can have a sexual type of relationship. And that was unusual and it caught me off guard, but I went ahead and said yes to it anyway as long as she understood that this is all it is."

Me: Did you ever question the paternity of your first child?

Big Tee: "Oh yes. I did of course, because during the pregnancy... while she was pregnant with my first child, she and the first baby dad still had some type relationship. Now to the extent of that relationship, I don't know. I have no earthly idea. I know him and some of his circumstances. He didn't have a car or whatever the situation was. I also knew that in their relationship, he was controlling in that relationship. So pretty much, what he told her to do and she did it. So if he said, 'hey come over here and pick me up and take me here,' then she would have done something like that.

"So that was the extent of that first relationship and I can believe that because when I was with her she liked... being controlled and I don't know if that stems back to... I felt like a lot of the problems we were having in our relationship, when we did have a relationship, cuz like I said it only lasted about 4 or 5 months, ummm were...I believe she was a compulsive liar as well. I believe it stems back to the fact that she tried to explain to me one day...and she wasn't a big talker. But how her dad raped her sister and it was out of the blue when she came to me with it and it was something that took place many years ago so ....when she was little. It's just something that made me think. Now it's just me thinking this, that it could have possibly been that her dad raped her and maybe that caused her to be as screwed up in the head as she is...trying to find relationships and trying to balance everything out in her head."

Me: You said she is screwed up in the head, you said she made you life hectic, how did she make your life hectic?

Big Tee: "The phrase....baby momma drama...I understand. I am very familiar with it. When my baby was a month old she took my baby (out of state), dropped her off came back to Memphis. I'm just like, 'where my daughter at?'
(Female) 'She's (out of state)...'
(Big Tee): 'Why is she (out of state)?'
(Female): 'Aww there's a specialist there she needs to see.'
(Big Tee) 'We have some of the best doctors around in Memphis. Why you drop her off (out of state)?'
A week later her sister called me and said, 'do you want your baby?'

(Big Tee): 'Huhh?'

(Female's sister): Yeah, you can come and get her.'

"She gave me the address. I left work that day. I drove 11 hours out of state and when I got there....my daughter was colicky as well she was premature, so when I got there like I said she was very little...I drove there with my sister...when I got there, everything that my daughter owned, everything I mean it filled up the bed of my truck.

"It's like (my child's mother) had lost her mind. She wasn't going to give me the baby and she didn't want the baby, so she tried to give the baby to her sister and had taken everything up there. A stroller... and my baby didn't even need a stroller at that time, I mean everything. I brought my daughter back home that night.

"When we got back to Memphis, she tried to call the police saying that I stolen my daughter, and umm, the lady was advising me to give her back to the mother. I am like, 'are yall crazy?' She just left my daughter out of state, but I had to do it... that was just at a month in.

"If I think back I can give you like a million and one stories of baby momma drama and unnecessary foolishness and I'm sure you have heard it a thousand times. Well that's just one side of the story...and maybe so, but we have spoken to her parents...

"She actually asked me to meet with her parents because she wasn't listening to me when I told her I didn't want to be with her. This was even after my daughter was born, and again, we did not mess off any while she was pregnant with my daughter. I found out my daughter was here three weeks after she was born.

"She called me up and was like, 'I had an abortion.'

"I was like, 'aww, for real?'

"She said, 'naw. I'm not going to be like that. Your daughter is here. She was born three weeks ago. If you want to come see her, you can come see her.'

"It was game after game, just a lot of foolishness."

Me: *How old was she at this point?*

Big Tee: "My daughter is 4."

Me: *How old was the mother when the child was born?*

Big Tee: "I wanna say like 27/28."

Me: At the birth of the child??

Big Tee: "Yeah."

Me: And how old were you??

Big Tee: "You know something? She was probably like 26, because I was 27/28."

Me: So who has custody of the child now?

Big Tee: "She has custody of her."

Me: So what is that relationship like?

Big Tee: "Well, umm, like I said, my daughter just turned four and I'm trying to pursue custody of her because I just feel like, I know what's best for my daughter and I'm interested in giving her what's best. The mother has accumulated so many children. I just don't feel like she can possibly be a better parent then I....I mean she has 5 now...."

Me: By how many men?

Big Tee: "To my knowledge, you know I really couldn't tell you. After that whole, this baby is yours thing, I just wanted to not know anything about what's going on. But I have heard from her co-workers and such that she said she wasn't going to stop until she has a boy and she has 5 girls now.

"I feel like a lot of that has to do with some issues that she needs to address.

"Getting back to the meeting with her parents, it was like I told her, 'hey look we can't be together. I don't want you.'

"I'm telling her these exact words. She said, 'you meet with my parents and I promise I will leave you alone about it.'

"We met with the parents. I tell the parents the same thing.... 'I'm not interested in your daughter. I don't want to be with her.'

"They tell her the same thing, she gets mad at them and starts cursing them out and leaves. The foolishness continues on.

"I didn't know the purpose of that meeting and I didn't know what she thought was gonna go down with that. But for me to tell her and her folks, and you still continue to pursue, it was just crazy to me. And this was all after the fact that you broke up with me....I don't care how you look at it. You broke up with me to see if with your first baby daddy was where you wanted be. So it was crazy…"

Me: What's your current relationship status?

Big Tee: "I'm married."

Me: How does that situation affect your marriage?

Big Tee: "For the most part, me and my wife we work as one. And my wife has a full understanding of how damaged (my oldest daughter's mother) is…We try, as long as I keep a full line of communication open with my wife to let her know what's going on… this is what she would like to go on…we are fine. If (my oldest daughter's mother) can try and find anything to poke her nose into and try to destroy, she will. She has 5 children and she said she has a fiancé and I hope so. But that still has not made her happy cuz she is still trying to get with me or have sexual relations with me."

Me: How does your wife feel about you pursuing custody of your oldest daughter?

Big Tee: "Well, my wife thinks that's best. She really doesn't want me to have anything to do with my baby's mama and if I had custody that wouldn't happen. So of course she wants me to pursue that."

Me: What were your expectations for the relationship?

Big Tee: "I told you man, rationally thinking, I shouldn't have done it. No woman in her right mind would tell you after you guys have dated, 'look. Check this out. Let's keep having sex'…So, I knew then that she was trying to get me trapped into something. She was trying to get back in with me. She was trying to buy time and I knew this. But I did it anyway because the sex was good… just to be honest with you the sex was good. I was interested in it and no strings attached. I mean literally I would call her at 1or 2 a.m. or she would call me at 1 or 2 a.m. and I would go do my do and I leave. So it was convenient, and at some point in time it got boring because I just knew it wasn't right. It wasn't the same because at one point we were actually in a relationship. Maybe I was trying to get even with her, I don't know…"

Me: What did you want? Did you strictly want just the sex?

Big Tee: "It was angry sex in the beginning. That was really funny to me… it was like I was just really dawging her out because I felt like she dawged me out. So since you asking for this, I'ma give it to you just like this, and she allowed me to dawg her out. And maybe that's what it was after I got that little revenge back, I felt a little guilty and I decided, 'okay. I'm done with this.' It was about a month I guess about a month and when I called and broke it off with her…that's when she hit me with she's was pregnant."

Me: What do you think she wanted?

Big Tee: "Again, that's the question I've been asking myself or the question I stopped asking myself, I guess a couple of years back …it's so crazy… it's just like now it seems like she wants me and she can't understand that she can't have me. Things have changed. I'm old fashioned like that…you know, after it's over with, it's over with…the way I feel about you that is… if I feel like I'm going to treat you like a queen…if I don't feel like you are a queen anymore, you can't go back and put that crown on your head. It doesn't mean anything. I'ma treat you like trash.

Me: So do you think she was using the sex…

Big Tee: "Of course. Definitely. Like I said, she was trying to buy time and hopefully the sex would be so good and so wonderful that I would be like, 'I want you back.' I tried to explain to her that I treated her like a queen before, not because of her sex, but because of who I am. She didn't understand that."

Me: How honest were you with her?

Big Tee: "I look back and if you are referring to back before my daughter was born…I look back and throughout that time I was honest. I came from a broken home myself. My mother had 5 children and no husband. No man was willing to step up to the plate and say, 'I am going to be your father. I'ma be that guy to take on this challenge of being your father.'
"I knew of a couple of men in my life that were willing to step up and take that challenge of raising children that were not (their biological children)…and again that's coming from the Klondike area, a poor community…so, I didn't see a lot of families. So when I met her, like I said we were working together, I knew that she had two kids but the way she portrayed the relationship was that she just had two kids and a baby

daddy that didn't really give a damn. I think that's what made me more intrigued than anything about the relationship because I knew if I dealt with her I am going deal with her and be straight up with her and do what I am supposed to do by her and those children. And that was the role I decided to take, not because of who she was, but because of who I am."

Me: Give me an example of being straight up with her and doing right by her and the children.

Big Tee: "Well, in my opinion, you just don't date a woman with kids unless you plan on actually pursuing something else with her. If you're just saying, 'okay. I'ma just cut.' Man, to me that's dirty.

"When a woman with children dates you, she's not looking for just a cut… nine times out of 10 she really wants a man, a male role model… that's my opinion. So that's what she's looking for so unless you are willing to step up, if things go the right way…unless you are willing to step up you shouldn't even mess with that situation. Or if you just looking at a situation saying that's easy ….then what you're doing… you dirty man."

Me: So basically, you could have seen that relationship progress to marriage?

Big Tee: "Ummm, I would have asked her to marry me. She wasn't homely, but like I said, because of the experiences I had in my life I felt proud to say that these aren't my children and I'm stepping up to the plate. You know what I'm sayin'…getting' it done. I look back and I have thought about this for quite some time about how my mother and some of the experiences she had…I still remember my mom talking to me and my sisters and looking at me and saying, 'you know…you gonna grow up and be a man one day and all men are dawgs.' So of course I wanted to prove my mama wrong and stuff. So, like I said, maybe it wasn't fair to her for me to take on that relationship because of my past, but I took it on and I knew I was gonna do right in that situation. If she wanted to pursue a marriage with me, we were definitely gonna have it.

Me: But, once you found out that she was seeing her other children's father, all that was out of the window?

Big Tee: "Yeah, once all that happened….I looked at her situation. She has two children and she out here playing games with people. I had none. I should be out here playing and so that's when I was like forget it."

Me: So how honest do you think she was with you?

Big Tee: "She wasn't honest at all. The person I know now, she is someone totally different than the person that I met when we got together. She didn't talk a lot, so I …its crazy to say this but she was more like ummm… I know you were taught the same thing I was….watch quiet people, them the ones you have to watch. Man she was extremely quiet. When I look back…after we broke up it took me literally two days to move on from that relationship. I remember one of my friends saying, 'man, how many kids she got?' I'm like, 'two.' (Friend) 'And how many you got?' I'm like, 'none.' We sat there and looked at each other for about two minutes, we laughed and I went on about my business. I was like… 'I'm back… I'm back.' Cuz it was her loss not mine, not mine. I'm the one that was willing to step up and do what a lot of men aren't, in my opinion. So it's your loss. That was a crazy situation for me."

Me: When did you guys start to have unprotected sex?

Big Tee: "Man, we started off from the rip…from the rip."

Me: How often?

Big Tee: "Every day for about 5 months."

Me: Everyday for about 5 months, unprotected sex?

Big Tee: "I promise you I'm not lying. Literally like every day. The majority of our relationship for her was spent in my bed. I would be like, 'come on. Let's take the two girls here or there.' A lot of the times it was just me and the two girls, when they weren't with their father. It was me and the two girls going out to Chuck E Cheese and stuff. All she wanted to do was sleep and fuck. It was great. She didn't talk. It wasn't…like I could say she was hiding anything… so it wasn't like you know…I couldn't say anything bad because it wasn't too much to say."

Me: What made you comfortable enough?

Big Tee: "To go bare?"

Me: Yeah.

Big Tee: "Sir, I was…(Pausing…) stupid. There is nothing else to say about it. I've been going bare. I started the relationship off and that was one of the reasons I like relationships. I like to go bare. I don't like wearing condoms, actually I hate 'em. So I figure if I get in this relationship, you on some protection, man I finna swang that thang. Looking back on it, I remember starting to pull a condom out. She looked at me and said, 'do you really have to use that?'

"'Nope!' I tossed that thing to the side and I been going bare ever since. So for five months straight I'm going bare and we break it off and come back and within a months' time, now all a sudden you finna get on swollen with a baby….I'm like man come on now. It just so happened the day I'm finna let you ride, I find out that this is what's up."

Me: Why did you question the paternity of the second child?

Big Tee: "Because it was one time that I started off with a condom and I don't think that I actually completed…I don't think that I (ejaculated) and I know you can get pregnant from (pre-ejaculation) or whatever. Man, I knew her to be someone totally different by that second child. She was an evil, conniving person and I did something that I wasn't supposed to that night. I went in and started to and said to myself, 'man this is your arch enemy. Why are you doing this? Let's roll on,' and I rolled on."

Me: How did that experience affect your view of women, dating and sex?

Big Tee: "Well, because it's her and she is the one woman I know to be like that, it didn't really change much with other women. I knew all the pitfalls before her, but I continued on….the only thing I can say is that if your first mind tells you don't do it ….go on and listen, go on and listen. Because my first mind told me don't do it…I still remember the first time that you know, I went on a date with her…I had the feeling like, 'man you probably shouldn't do this'. …but even though I knew that if I was going to do it, I had to be man enough to step up to the plate, but it was just something that said….man don't do that."

Me: What stands out as the most valuable lesson you learned from the whole experience?

Big Tee: "My daughter is 4 now and this woman is still trying to cause hell in my life. I know that the relationship… I've been blessed enough that any and everything I didn't like in a woman in a relationship, I could leave at any point in time no matter what goes on. I could leave…this woman aint gone. When you make a baby this woman is really tied to you and it can be like a prison in a sense that you have to deal with this person for x amount of years of your life… if I could go back and do it again….I wouldn't have done it… heck naw. But I love my daughter more then I dislike her. She didn't feel the same way. All she feels is pain she feels I caused and she doesn't care who else hurts. So if she can hurt my daughter to hurt me then she would."

Me: How do you deal with that?

Big Tee: "I stay prayerful. I have too. I remember when we went to court the judge talked to me as if I hadn't taken care of my daughter and I'm not a father, just another black man down here trying to get over as opposed to somebody who's been trying to take care of their child. I remember how I felt when I left that court and I remember while we were there, again, she told me if I just date her….take her out on a couple of dates, that she would not take me to court…that's the only reason we went to court because I said no…and I was in a relationship at the time too.

Me: How can these situations be prevented?

Big Tee: Know your intent. We all know preventive measures of dealing in relationships, especially sexual relationships when it comes to children. I feel like the majority of my pain was caused because I didn't do right. I knew that I shouldn't have been sleeping with this woman especially without a condom…I knew this and I did it anyway. The pain that came with the baby mama drama from baby one and the pain she tried to inflict from baby two…all these things took place because, hey, I wasn't smart enough to use a condom and I did something that was against my will. I think about it a lot, if I had just done things the way Christ intended, how much easier my life would have been. No sex without marriage. I know it sounds crazy to some people but think about how much pain you prevent. It's fun when you are doing it, but when you have to pay the piper it's not much fun then.

Me: Do you have any additional comments?

Big Tee: Don't be in such a rush to have fun…take a little time out. That fun can equal a lot of pain.

My Reflection after Big Tee's Interview

My office (The University of Memphis)

June 1, 2010

I was surprised by the fact that Big Tee had unprotected sex with his former partner, who was not on birth control, everyday from the beginning of the relationship and that they went on that way for approximately five months. He was nearly 30 years old when they met and many of the guys I know use condoms regularly by that age.

I do know a few guys, though, that openly admit how much they hate condoms. They usually complain that the condoms aren't comfortable. In those cases, guys might keep a steady girlfriend with whom they trust to be faithful and use birth control so they can have sex without a condom.

One of the oldest tricks in the book for women who intend to keep men in relationships by getting pregnant is to tell her sex partner that she is on birth control when in reality she is not. In the streets the child is referred to as the "keep-a-man baby" because the child was conceived in an effort to keep her sex partner in her life. Big Tee's case is not the typical "keep-a-man baby" because Big Tee said he knew his partner was not using any type of birth control.

I personally dealt with a situation in college where I became so comfortable with a girl friend that we agreed to have unprotected sex. She said she was on birth control, but still became pregnant somehow. She told me that she forgot to take her pill one day and became pregnant as a result of missing that one pill.

I remember talking to my college advisor about the situation. My advisor, Dr. Hopson, knew about the paternity case I dealt with as a freshman in college and gave me sound advice following that tragedy. I was embarrassed to walk into her office two years later with a similar situation, but I felt like she would be able to help me.

I could see the disappointment on Dr. Hopson's face when I told her the news. She dropped her head for a moment then literally shook it off before she started talking. I told her that the girl and I had a strong relationship and I trusted that she was taking her birth control faithfully.

Dr. Hopson told me that I had to take responsibility for myself and that my future was not someone else's responsibility. I felt stupid and I was embarrassed, but she was right. I was in no position to blame anyone but myself for the consequences of my own actions. Big Tee never blamed his former sex partner for the pregnancy during the interview. He said his actions were stupid.

Another interesting aspect of Big Tee's interview was the fact that he felt it was a badge of honor to date, with view to marriage, a woman with children. He said in his interview that his mother raised him and his siblings without a permanent male figure in the home. The lack of a male role model encouraged Big Tee to be the role model as an adult that he lacked as a child.

It seemed that Big Tee might have been more attracted to the idea of being the man that his father was not than the idea of getting to know the woman he said he could have seen himself marrying. He said he would take her children on outings while his girlfriend at the time would stay home. Although it was a noble gesture to reach out to his lover's children, Big Tee might have set himself up for heartache by trying to develop a family before developing a functional relationship with the woman he was having sex with.

Epilogue

Both Chip and Big Tee said they were able to rebound and move on without bitterness and vengeful spirits. Chip is still playing his saxophone. He also plans to go back to college and finish his music degree. He has a steady girlfriend to whom he said is faithful.

Big Tee is happily married with a daughter.

Eric and Dre expressed anger, bitterness and distrust after their situations. I felt those same emotions.

Eric remains consumed with his business. He now owns three companies in Memphis. He said he was still bitter and distrustful of women during his interview, less than three years removed from his paternity test results. He is single.

Dre eventually calmed his rage and married approximately eight years after receiving his paternity test results. His wife is pregnant with a daughter.

I married and divorced. I was very distrusting and paranoid during my marriage. I hope to be able to trust a woman's word again one day, but I don't know if I will ever be able to fully do that. I plan to have a paternity test with any children I might be credited with fathering in the future, even if I am married.

People heal differently.

Afterword

What are common experiences shared among men who were falsely credited with paternity?

There were several common experiences among the men who shared their narratives. Several aspects of the relations were different as well.

The men and women worked together in two of the narratives. One couple started as schoolmates who were connected by mutual friends. One couple met at a night club and I met the girl in my narrative while I was working in the mall and she was shopping.

Four of the five relationships were categorized as casual dating by the male narrators. Only Eric's case was a story where both parties claimed to be monogamous, even though Eric openly admitted that he cheated, but thought his girlfriend was faithful. Chip knew that his sex partner had a boyfriend from the beginning. Big Tee's relationship status changed once his sex partner left him for an old boyfriend. Dre said his partner knew he dated other women his age and there was never a monogamous commitment in my relationship either.

Three of the five men said they were not looking for long term relationships with the women they were involved with sexually. Big Tee said he saw his sex partner as a potential marriage mate initially. Still, their relationship had transformed from exclusive to purely sexual during the period when she became pregnant with the child she falsely accused Big Tee of conceiving. Eric said he saw his high school sweetheart potentially becoming his wife.

The relationships were all traditional in terms of contemporary dating structure. The couples went to movies and shared meals and conversations. My case was different initially. We phone-dated because our parents did not know about our relationship.

Chip and Dre both said their relationships provided fun, stress-free atmospheres. Eric found security and stability in having a girlfriend while Big Tee was only in it for the sex the second time around. My relationship provided freshness from what I was accustomed to.

Chip, Dre and Big Tee said their relationships provided their female counterparts with security in knowing they had a good guy. I felt the same way in hindsight. Eric said he felt like his girlfriend's self-esteem was boosted by means of their relationship because of his popularity in high school.

What are the relationships between trust and sexual interactions?

Eric was the only man who said he was not totally honest in his relationship with his sexual partner. Chip, Dre, Big Tee and I said we had no reason to lie to the women we dated because the relationships were not monogamous.

All narrators called the honesty of the women they dealt with into question due to the paternity incidents. Dre and Eric said they thought the women they dated were totally honest before the false paternity accusations. I had no reason to believe the girl I was intimate with had ever lied to me either. Big Tee said he never really got to know the woman who falsely accused him of paternity because she was usually quiet and their relationship consisted mostly of sex. Chip said he knew his sex partner was dishonest from the beginning.

Three of the five men willingly participated in unprotected sex with their partners. Chip said he wore a condom that busted during intercourse, and I used a condom in the one event I had sex with my partner before she became pregnant. Big Tee said he and his partner had unprotected sex every day for approximately five months before she became pregnant with his oldest daughter and he had unprotected sex with her again before she became pregnant with her fourth child. Eric estimated having unprotected sex two out of every three times with his partner, and Dre estimated he and his partner had unprotected sex one out of every five times.

Eric and Dre said they were comfortable to have unprotected sex with their partners because they relaxed after dating for some time. Big Tee said his case was simple stupidity while Chip and I had no intention of engaging in unprotected sex.

Birth control was only mentioned as a factor with Big Tee. Dre said his partner told him she was unable to have children due to a medical condition. Eric practiced the pull-out method in which the male withdraws his penis from the female's vagina just before the point of ejaculation.

Chip did not question the paternity of the child he was falsely accused of fathering. He said he believed the child was his son because a condom busted at the point of ejaculation around the time his sex partner became pregnant. Dre said he planned to get a paternity test, but failed to do so initially because he was busy with college. He said he felt like he could be the child's father because of the regularity with which he and his ex-girlfriend had unprotected sex. Eric said he believe the child his ex-girlfriend was carrying was his son all the way until the boy's birth. He said he had a feeling at the hospital that he was not the child's father. Big Tee said he was convinced he was not the child's father because he did not fully ejaculate into his partner. I felt I was not the father of the child in my narrative because her mother and I only had sex one time and I used a condom that did not bust or come off.

Each man received DNA evidence through paternity tests that he was not the father of the child in question. Four of the five men initiated their own paternity tests with the women that falsely accused them of paternity. Chip was the only man who did not. Another man who was having sex with Dre's partner initiated the case that revealed he was not the father of the child he thought was his son. My father and Dre's father stepped in to encourage us to get paternity tests while Eric and Big Tee took the initiative on their own.

How did your experience then transfer to your life now?

Dre said his views of women, dating and sex were damaged dramatically. He said he began disrespecting women and using them as sexual objects once he found out he had been lied to about the child's paternity. Years later, Dre married the next woman he seriously dated. Eric said he lost trust in the human race, not just women. He said he is skeptical of true love and the possibility of a happy marriage. My view of dating and relationships was headed in a negative direction after I was cheated on by a high school girlfriend. The paternity situation didn't make things any better. I seriously question the motives of women who attempt to have intimate relationships with me. Big Tee said he would not let his negative incident have a negative impact on his intimate relationships and is happily married. Chip said he won't let his past determine his future.

Eric encouraged others to follow their hearts after his experience. He said he had no reason to doubt the paternity of the child his ex-girlfriend birthed, but a feeling in his heart edged him to do so. Dre encouraged anyone with a doubt to get tested as well. Big Tee said he learned to appreciate that a child is a commitment and calls for a lasting relationship with the child's mother, whether the father likes it or not. Chip said he learned to value his own inner strength following his ordeal. He said he feels he can rise to any occasion after stepping up to be a father in his early

20s. I learned to appreciate the value of life just a little more. I thought I might have brought a new life into the world, then I witnessed someone very close to me lose her life. We have to be careful about creating life and appreciate our own.

Chip said honesty and discretion when choosing sex partners could prevent situations like what he experienced. Eric said prospective fathers should follow their heart. Dre said using condoms and knowing the person you are sleeping with is the answer. Big Tee said sexually active individuals should know their intentions in their relationships and take preventive measures when it comes to sex. I say be careful and think.

Chapter 6
Conclusions

The couples meeting in different ways suggests how two people meet does not dictate paternity. There is a misconception that relationships born in night clubs or bars will not be successful, but meeting people through mutual friends is better. Although Dre had a tragic experience with a girl he met at a night club, Eric met his girlfriend through mutual friends and the relationship ended much the same.

There is no specific relationship scenario that dictates false paternity claims. Narratives in this book came from men in supposedly exclusive boyfriend/girlfriend relationships, open dating arrangements and strictly sexual scenarios. The variation in relationship circumstances suggests that a false paternity accusation can come from any type relationship. A person could be sadly mistaken to believe he is the father of a child simply because his girlfriend is pregnant. Although a boyfriend might believe his girlfriend has not had sex with another man, he could be wrong.

The narratives also suggest that knowing your intent is only half the battle. Eric and Big Tee both saw the women that falsely accused them of paternity as potential future wives. Although those two men might have started with honorable intentions, they were still falsely accused of paternity. It would be reasonable to think the women knew they were dating men who wanted to be with them long-term and lied to them in order to keep them in their lives when they got pregnant by other men. Dre and I did not express the thought of pursuing an extended future with the women we dated, but we were lied to as well. It would be reasonable to assume that the women were using their pregnancy as a tactic to keep us included in their lives because they felt we would be better fathers than the actual biological parent. In Chip's case, he was initially told he was the father and assumed financial responsibility until the natural father demanded a paternity test. It is safe to assume Chip's sex partner wanted him to be the father as well.

Men have to understand that pregnant women are in complicated situations when they have had multiple sex partners near the time of conception. There is no way she can be sure who the father of her child is, no matter how convincing she might sound. Knowing that family, friends and society as a whole could look down at her if she admits she has been promiscuous, it is often more convenient to tell a lie and stick to it.

All the relationships provided positive atmospheres initially as well. Aside from Big Tee's situation, none of the cases were negative until the issues of pregnancy and paternity. Some people might mistakenly believe that baby mama drama or false paternity accusations are situations reserved for dysfunctional relationships, but that is not the case. Eric and Dre especially were involved in healthy, functional relationships where they got along fine with their sex partners and they were falsely accused of paternity nonetheless.

Being honest with your sex partner does not mean your sex partner is being honest with you. Four of the five men in the narratives said they were totally honest with their sex partners. All five men were lied to, though. One of the five women in the book eventually told the truth. And she did so after having received paternity results from a test with another sex partner. All five men, women and children involved could still be living lies today had no one ever taken a paternity test.

Engaging in unprotected sex does not equal paternity. Big Tee had unprotected sex with his partner around the time she got pregnant, but was not the father of her child. Eric and Dre regularly had unprotected sex with their partners, but were not the fathers of their children. Eric and Dre thought they impregnated those women because they had unprotected sex with them, but the paternity test showed otherwise.

All five narrators said they learned valuable lessons from their experiences and I will leave you with those: from Chip, be honest and use discretion when choosing sex partners; from Eric, follow your heart; from Dre, use condoms and know the person with whom you are sleeping; from Big Tee, know your intentions and take preventive measures; from me, be careful and think.

About the Author

I've been a writer for as long as I can remember. I wrote poems and read them to my friends and classmates in the second and third grade.

My writing became therapy for me when I began to notice domestic tension between my parents in the early 1990s. I would write about my feelings: happiness, sadness, confusion, pain. I was recognized by teachers and students at Westside High School in Memphis as one of the top writers in the school by my sophomore year. I would write dedication poems for schools events and programs.

I joined the inaugural staff of Teen Appeal in 1997. Teen Appeal is a citywide high school newspaper program involving The Scripps Howard Foundation, The Commercial Appeal, The University of Memphis and Memphis City Schools. I worked as a reporter and photographer during my senior year in high school and earned a journalism scholarship to the University of Memphis.

As an undergraduate student at Memphis I served as a reporter and editor for *The Daily Helmsman.* I worked as a sports intern at the *Birmingham Post-Herald* in Summer 2002 and for *The Associated Press* as an editorial assistant in Spring 2002. I also interned with the NBA's Memphis Grizzlies as a media relations associate and wrote for their site, www.grizzlies.com, in 2001 following an internship with *The Commercial Appeal* as a sports intern in 2000.

Prior to graduation I received the University of Memphis Journalism Department Newspaper/Editorial Student of the Year 2003 Award and the National Association of Black Journalists U of M Chapter, Excellence Award in Sports Writing in 2003.

Still, with all the accolades I had earned, I felt like I had not done enough. I wanted to tell deeper stories. One of my favorite quotes from author Byron Lopez says, "The stories people tell have a way of taking care of them. If stories come to you take care of them. And learn to give them away when they are needed. Sometimes a person needs a story - more than food to stay alive."

The thought that I might help someone by sharing trials I have persevered through makes me think the trial might have been worthwhile. I want to give stories away now.

I earned a master's degree in Instruction and Curriculum Leadership from the University of Memphis in 2008 and was accepted to the doctoral program in Higher and Adult Education at the U of M the following semester.

I used school as an excuse not to chase my dream of being a professional writer instead of a platform to accomplish that dream. Family and friends have been asking when I would release my first book since I was an undergraduate student and I always put them off by saying I would drop several books after graduation. A lecture and advice from film maker Spike Lee about using our resources inspired me to create an artwork this summer.

Lee told a recent University of Memphis graduate, 'you don't go to film school to learn how to make films,' in his lecture. He added. 'You go to film school to get access to what you need to make films.'

Lee lectured in the Rose Theatre at The University of Memphis April of 2010. He talked about the action necessary to make things happen and said that waiting on other people to live out your dreams for you is not the answer. His talk inspired me personally.

Initially I was going to direct a short film, but my younger brother Gregory encouraged me to write a book. He told me I had been a writer all my life and I should use my gift to my advantage. The next step was to decide what I would write about.

I plan to release an autobiography when I finish my doctorate in education in 2012. Although I've experienced enough joy and tragedy to write an autobiography already, I feel people will be more interested in hearing my entire life story once I have the doctor's credential.

Manufactured By: RR Donnelley
Breinigsville, PA USA
August, 2010